YO-YO DOLLS
& DOLL QUILTS

Bobbie
McClure
Long

American Quilter's Society
P. O. Box 3290 • Paducah, KY 42002-3290
www.AmericanQuilter.com

Located in Paducah, Kentucky, the American Quilter's Society (AQS) is dedicated to promoting the accomplishments of today's quilters. Through its publications and events, AQS strives to honor today's quiltmakers and their work and to inspire future creativity and innovation in quiltmaking.

EXECUTIVE BOOK EDITOR: ANDI MILAM REYNOLDS
SENIOR BOOK EDITOR: LINDA BAXTER LASCO
GRAPHIC DESIGN: ELAINE WILSON
COVER DESIGN: MICHAEL BUCKINGHAM
PROJECT PHOTOGRAPHY: CHARLES R. LYNCH
HOW-TO PHOTOGRAPHY: BOBBIE MCCLURE LONG

Additional copies of this book may be ordered from the American Quilter's Society, PO Box 3290, Paducah, KY 42002-3290, or online at www.AmericanQuilter.com.

Text © 2010, Author, Bobbie McClure Long
Artwork © 2010, American Quilter's Society

Library of Congress Cataloging-in-Publication Data

Long, Bobbie McClure.
  Yo-yo dolls & doll quilts / by Bobbie McClure Long.
    p. cm.
  ISBN 978-1-57432-663-5
  1. Dollmaking. 2. Patchwork--Patterns. 3. Doll quilts. I. Title.
  TT175.L65 2010
  745.592'21--dc22
                                    2010006249

American Quilter's Society
P. O. Box 3290 • Paducah, KY 42002-3290
www.AmericanQuilter.com

DEDICATION

It is with gratitude, love, honor, and pride that I dedicate this book to the women of great talent, intelligence, and poise who came before me: my grandmothers, Mary DeShong McClure and Martha Ellen Francis Riggs; my mom, Mary Jane Riggs McClure; and aunt, Wilma Riggs Coffield.

And to the creative, smart, and confident women who have come after me: my daughters Trish Hackett, Crista Mehringer, Megan Wohlberg, and Mallory Goodman; and their daughters Katie, Maddie, and Allie Hackett; Sydney Wohlberg; and Rylee and Sienna Mehringer—the next generation of young women whose futures are filled with opportunities that their great-great-grandmothers could have never imagined.

To my dad, Robert DeShong McClure, the greatest dad ever. His ability to find the best in everything endeared him to everyone and enabled him to live a long, admirable, accomplished life.

To my husband, Thomas Schultz Long, who walks hand in hand with me through life and into places few men dare to go—fabric stores and quilt shows. His encouragement, suggestions, insight, and patience were invaluable in making this book possible. He is my best friend, my confidant, and dance partner. He is the man I love and cherish with all my heart.

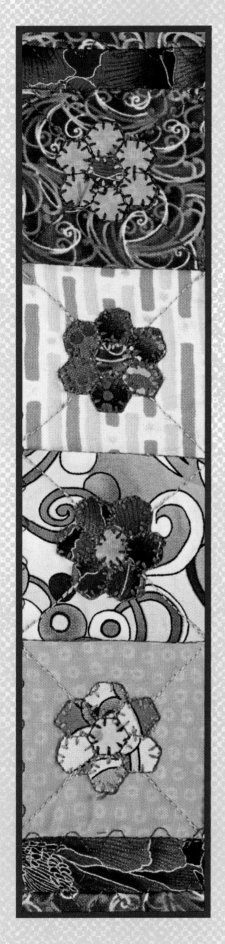

ACKNOWLEDGMENTS

I would like to give special thanks to my large blended family and my friends, especially my grandchildren who say, and mistakenly think, "Grandma can do anything."

To all the members of The Pocono Mountain Quilters' Guild for their friendship, instruction, encouragement, and support.

To East Stroudsburg University of Pennsylvania for making me get out of my comfort zone and out of my own way and for reminding me of the joy of lifelong learning.

CAROLYN'S GARDEN, 9½" x 9½", made by the author, instructions on page 40.

CONTENTS

9NTRODUCTION

Each one of the dolls is made just a little differently, but they are all made out of the same stuff. Like people, no two are exactly the same. Even using the photographs as a guide, every yo-yo doll's face will look just a little bit different. The buttons you use for the eyes, the exact placement of them, where you put the nose, and the tightness of the stitches you use in outlining their smiles subtly change their look. The faces on the dolls, their hair color and cut, and the fabric in the yo-yos are there for you to use as a guide. You will create your own doll's personality by the way you put everything together.

Once you have made one doll, you will see how easy they are to make. Individual instructions for each doll will give the specifics for that particular doll. Patterns for the dolls are in the back of the book. Auntie Em, Mary Ellen, Victoria, and Carolyn all use the same pattern. Sam and Jake use the same pattern. Charlie and Willa Jane each have their own patterns, as do Missy and Juno, the cat and dog.

Fabric thickness is a big factor in determining how many yo-yos are on each doll. For example, Victoria has fewer yo-yos because velvet fabric is thicker than the cotton fabric used in the other yo-yo dolls. The fabrics you choose may have different thicknesses than the ones used in the book. If that is the case, you will see as you slip the yo-yos on the dolls' bodies that the number of yo-yos you use may change a little. See specific instruc-

tions for the number of yo-yos used in each doll and for hair, shoes, and other details.

There's a list of the basic yo-yo doll supplies used in making all the dolls (page 11) that you should have on hand. Please read the instructions and list of materials and supplies specific to each doll before beginning. Generally, the fabrics used in making the little quilts are scraps left over from making the dolls.

All seams are ¼" unless otherwise stated. The yo-yos closest to the body have the stitching sides facing in toward the center of the doll. The yo-yos facing the hands, feet, and head have the stitching sides facing out away from the body.

Experience the joy of finishing an entire quilt, start-to-finish, in just a day or two by using fabric scraps! Only Sam's little quilt, BEAR COUNTRY, has some hand quilting. The rest are quilted by machine and many use those fancy little stitches that have been hiding in your sewing machine waiting to be used for something.

The yo-yo dolls and their little quilts are easy enough for a beginner and creative enough for an experienced quilter to enjoy. After you get the hang of making them, experiment! Let your imagination go on a field trip! There are as many possibilities as there are fabrics at your local quilt shop!

HISTORY OF YO-YOS

Tracking the history of the fabric yo-yo is as time consuming as making a yo-yo doll! Many people have different ideas about its origin. I could not find a complete history on yo-yos anywhere. This is what I discovered and surmised from reading different blogs on the Internet where people commented on what they were told and what they remembered from childhood.

The earliest known fabric yo-yos seem to have been made in the nineteenth century. Yo-yos made of velvet and lace adorn Victorian crazy quilts. These yo-yos were sometimes called puffs or Marguerites. Cotton yo-yos became very popular in the United States in the 1920s, '30s, and '40s. The ability to carry all you needed to make a yo-yo anywhere you went made them a popular pastime and I would guess many fabric circles were traded among friends. This could explain the examples of scrappy yo-yo quilts made with many different feedsack fabrics in one quilt.

Some people think the popularity of the fabric yo-yo grew with the popularity of the yo-yo toy. The wooden toy was very popular in the1930s and 1940s as well but goes back in history to ancient societies. It was thought to be used as a hunting weapon as well as a gift given to the gods.

Yo-yo dolls seem to have come onto the scene in the 1950s. Most were clowns with a preformed plastic face from a 5 & 10 Cent store. They were made with long floppy, dangly arms and legs that were held together with strong string. They had bells on the ends of the arms and legs. In the 1960s the faces were made of fabric and elephants, bunnies, dogs, cats, owls, caterpillars, and just about anything else you could think of started to appear.

Today, yo-yos are making a comeback. The yo-yo dolls in this book start a new chapter with the idea that it's what's inside that counts. Like yo-yo projects that came before them, they are a still a portable quilting project for busy people.

The oldest toy in the world is the doll. The toy wooden yo-yo is said to be the second oldest toy in the world. Quilters have combined the two and created a doll assembled from fabric yo-yos and made the yo-yo doll the classic quilter's doll.

MEET THE YO-YO FAMILY

The yo-yo family has eight members— Mary Ellen, Auntie Em, Victoria, Carolyn, Sam, Jake, Charlie, and Willa Jane. Just like any other family they are similar in many ways and you can see a family resemblance. But they are all individuals, with each member having their own style and attitude. They are a family, just like yours or mine.

Mary Ellen

Mary Ellen is dear to my heart because she is named after my mother (Mary Jane) and both my grandmothers (Ella and Mary). She's a little particular and always wears her pearls when she is dressed up. She likes to dress for success. She is a modern, stylish woman who knows what she wants and works hard to achieve it. Her namesakes would be very pleased with the combining of the old and new techniques in her little yo-yo quilt, Yo-Yos All in a Row.

Auntie Em

Auntie Em—every family has one, from Dorothy in *The Wizard of Oz* to this yo-yo family. Some are more conservative than the yo-yo Auntie Em, but the common characteristic is how much they share. This Auntie Em is a lot of fun to make and one of the easiest dolls to make because her whole "outfit" is one fabric. Auntie Em is a little flashier than the rest of her family and rhinestones twinkle from her stylish glasses. She is all dressed up in leopard fabric yo-yos, complete with beads and a boa. She has her funky Log Cabin tiger quilt, Kansas City Here I Come, packed and ready to go on a road trip.

Victoria likes all things Victorian. She wears blue velvet and lace, a crystal necklace, and a rose on the lace collar at her neck. Her beautiful brown wavy hair hangs loosely around her face and down her back with a small bun at the back of her head adorned with three roses. Rhinestones decorate the buttons on her velvet shoes that she wears over white satin stockings. She likes to cozy up next to the wood stove in the parlor while she lovingly adds more stitches onto her crazy VICTORIA'S QUILT.

Blue is **Carolyn's** favorite color and she is dressed in shades of it from head to toe. Even her stylish beads and matching bracelet are blue. Her bright aqua socks peek out from behind the bows on her blue shoes. Carolyn loves to work in her garden in the spring and summer. She is a quilter during the winter months. So, of course, she appliquéd flowers on the quilt she named CAROLYN'S GARDEN.

Sam likes the mountains. His fishing cabin is where he likes to be. He is most comfortable at his little lake with a fishing pole or hiking in the woods enjoying nature. Sam is an outdoorsman. He would much rather dress in his plaid shirt, blue jeans, and hiking boots than a business suit. In the evening he likes to kick back in front of the fireplace in BEAR COUNTRY.

Jake is an intellectual—from his tortoiseshell glasses to his khaki pants. He likes bright colors and he likes to stand out in a crowd. He loves sports and likes to play a round of golf whenever he can. He always feels lucky when he sees the pair of bald eagles in their nest high above the golf course along the Delaware River. The colorful quilt GEESE OF MANY COLORS Carolyn made is just right for him.

Charlie is the boy in the yo-yo family. He is a Pittsburgh Steelers fan. He likes to wear the yellow and black colors the Steelers wear. His black baseball cap even has the Steelers logo on it. He sleeps under his STELLAR STEELERS quilt every night and dreams of becoming a great football player.

Willa Jane is the little girl of the family—the baby. She is a little sweetie in ribbons and bows. She is named after my very favorite aunt, Aunt Wilma, and my mom, Mary Jane. She loves the stories in the *Tales of Peter Rabbit*. Her favorite Potter is Beatrix; she doesn't even know who Harry Potter is! That is why Willa Jane's mother named her daughter's little quilt THE OTHER POTTER.

Many families have pets and the yo-yo family is no exception. Missy the cat and Juno the dog are part of this family, too.

Juno is our granddog. She is a lot smaller and is not as vocal or as lively as her namesake, but she does articulate! She is a chubby little puppy that can sit up and beg for you to pet her soft fur.

Missy is soft and furry. You can tell a lot about cats by what they do with their tails. So Missy's tail articulates and turns up or down as she continues on in her imaginative adventures.

Tools Make the Person

Tools and Supplies

I recommend the Clover® circle-shape "Quick" Yo-Yo Makers. They come in 5 sizes and are worth their weight in gold! The yo-yos are always perfect.

Clover "Quick" Yo-Yo Maker – Jumbo (blue)
Clover "Quick" Yo-Yo Maker – Extra Large (yellow)
Clover "Quick" Yo-Yo Maker – Large (orange)
Clover "Quick" Yo-Yo Maker – Small (green)
Clover "Quick" Yo-Yo Maker – Extra Small (blue)

In addition, you should have the following tools and notions on hand to make the yo-yo dolls. Finishing touches such as rivets, fringe, rhinestones, assorted beads, ribbons, glasses, baseball cap logo, and exact colors and sizes are specified in the patterns.

HeatnBond® Light Weight Iron-On Fusible Interfacing
Light and dark upholstery thread
(for making the yo-yos)
Sewing needles
Doll needles
Dritz® Fray Check® sealant
Polyester fiberfill
Yarn for hair
Covered buttons for noses
Buttons for eyes
Stretchy jewelry cord
Embroidery or craft thread
Black fine-line permanent marker
Assorted fabric pens *(pink for lips, black and brown for eyebrows)*
Pink scrapbooking chalk
Chalking puffs or Q-tips®
Dark pink craft paint *(for lips)*
Fabric medium *(for lips)*
Fabric glue
Wooden spoon with a wide handle
(for stuffing)

Other helpful but optional items:

Eleanor Burns' Mini Geese One ruler
(for Jake's quilt)
Awl
Polyester craft trim *(for Auntie Em's scarf)*
¼" bias-tape maker *(for Mary Ellen's quilt)*

INNER STRENGTH IS IMPORTANT

Making the Doll Body

Cut all pattern pieces with the arrow on the fabric straight-of-grain.

Trace and cut out the pattern pieces.

Trace the pieces onto ivory or brown fabric and cut out 2 bodies, 2 heads, and 4 hands.

Sew the pieces right sides together with a ¼" seam allowance.

Leave the bottom of the neck on the head and the wrists on the hands open. Leave an opening on one side of the body from armpit to hip. Backstitch at the beginning and end of the openings.

Turn right-side out using an unsharpened pencil or commercial fabric turner. Stuff firmly with fiberfill. Be sure to get fiberfill in the thumb. Slipstitch the body opening closed and set aside (Fig. 1).

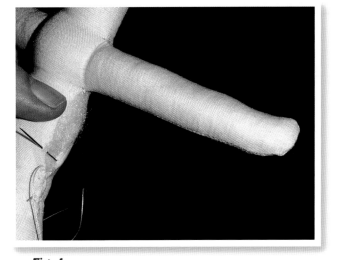

Fig. 1

Making the Face

Make a hole in the center of the doll's face using a small awl or large needle; apply Fray Check sealant and let dry.

Make one covered button from a matching fabric scrap following the manufacturer's instructions.

Sew the button nose on the face allowing the shank of the button to rest in the hole made by the awl. Sew from the front to the back of the head. (Don't worry. The hair and/or hat will cover stitch marks.)

On the colored buttons used for eyes, make a black circle around the buttonholes with a black fine-line permanent pen. Color in the circle (for the pupil of the eyes).

Referring to the photograph of the doll, sew on the buttons for the doll's eyes. Both buttons for each eye can be sewn on at the same time. Add a 2mm rhinestone to each eye to give the doll twinkling eyes.

Add eyebrows with a fabric pen. (Don't worry, everyone's eyebrows are not exactly the same.)

Copy lips from the photograph with a fine-line fabric marker. Then make small stitches with matching thread from the back of the head coming through to the front, outlining the lines you made with a fabric marker. This will give the lips some dimension.

The doll's head, hands, and the shoes and socks will be attached after yo-yos are on the doll. Hair will be attached after the head is sewn to the body. See specific pattern instructions for details.

Hint: If you are not happy with the lips, mix a little craft paint of your choice with craft fabric medium (follow the directions on the fabric medium bottle) and lightly go over the lips with a very small paint brush to get the look you want.

MAKING YO-YOS

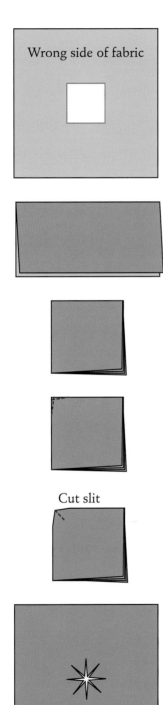

Wrong side of fabric

Cut slit

The body, leg, and arm yo-yos have an opening for the body parts to go through. This hole is reinforced with fusible interfacing. I use HeatnBond Light Weight Iron-On Fusible Interfacing. No hole is cut in the socks and shoes yo-yos, so they do not need the interfacing.

❁ Cut fabric squares as specified in the pattern. Cut smaller squares of interfacing and fuse onto the center of the wrong side of the fabric squares, following the manufacturer's instructions.

❁ Fold the fused squares in half twice and cut a small star-shaped hole at the folded corner.

❁ Remove the paper backing.

❁ Proceed with making the yo-yos (page 15), either with the Clover Yo-Yo Makers or by the traditional method.

❁ For traditional yo-yos, trace a circle the diameter of the square size specified in the pattern. (Traditionally, you cut a circle twice the size of the yo-yo you want to make and add ¼" seam allowance.)

❁ Cut out the circle and fold under the seam allowance.

❁ Knot a length of upholstery thread or doubled sewing thread and sew a running stitch around the circle through the folded edge.

❁ Overlap the first stitch with the last stitch and gently pull the thread to gather your circle into a yo-yo.

❁ Do not cinch closed the yo-yos used for the socks and those closest to the head and hands. Leave an 8" tail of thread for cinching them up after they are added to the dolls. For all the other yo-yos, pull the thread, leaving an opening about ½" across, and secure with a couple of backstitches. Knot and trim the thread.

YO-YOS DRESS THE DOLL

Specific measurements, amounts, and finishing touches are given with each doll pattern. The techniques for adding yo-yos to the doll's body are the same. The Charlie and Willa Jane yo-yos will be a size smaller than specified here and the Bobbie Doll yo-yos will be one size larger. Refer to the yo-yo chart in each pattern for placement of the yo-yos.

Making the Yo-Yos

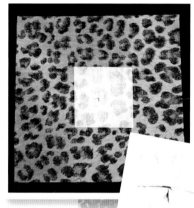

⊗ Cut strips of fabric into squares.

⊗ Cut smaller squares of HeatnBond.

⊗ Fuse the interfacing to the center of the fabric squares following the manufacturer's instructions.

⊗ Fold the fabric square in half twice to find the middle. Snip a ¼" long sliver off the edges of the folds and make a ¼" long snip on the diagonal to cut a star shape in the middle. Peel the paper off the interfacing (Fig. 1).

Fig. 1

⊗ Insert the fabric square into the yo-yo maker and follow the manufacturer's instructions. I recommend using light or dark upholstery thread when making the yo-yos.

Dressing the Body
Torso

⊗ Put the first jumbo yo-yo on the doll's arm, then over the neck and the other arm (like putting on a shirt).

⊗ Pull the yo-yo all the way down so it rests low on the doll's hips (Fig. 2).

⊗ In the same way, continue stacking yo-yos on the body until they reach the armpits. You may need more or fewer yo-yos than specified in the pattern, depending on your fabrics.

Fig. 2

Fig. 3

Fig. 4

Fig. 5

Fig. 6   Fig. 7

Neck and Head

✪ Put one jumbo yo-yo on the neck above arms.

✪ Slipstitch the neck yo-yo to the yo-yo that is under the arms (Fig. 3).

✪ Put an extra-large and large yo-yo on the neck. The large yo-yo closest to the head is not cinched.

✪ Put the head on the neck. To secure the head, slipstitch around the bottom of the head by inserting the needle through the neck, front to back and side to side.

✪ Pull the top uncinched yo-yo up to where the head is attached, and cinch closed to cover the stitches on the doll's neck.

Legs

✪ Put an extra-large yo-yo on the doll's right leg; pull it up to the hips. Repeat on the left leg.

✪ Slipstitch the two leg yo-yos together, then sew them to the first jumbo yo-yo you put on the torso (Figs. 4 and 5).

✪ Put cinched yo-yos on the legs down to the ankles.

✪ Put uncinched ankle yo-yos on each of the doll's legs. Do not cinch them yet.

Socks

✪ To make the socks, stuff two uncut yo-yos with polyester fiberfill. Leave room in the middle of each sock for the leg (*a space about the size of your index finger*) (Fig. 6).

✪ Slip the socks onto each leg and cinch shut. Secure them by sewing back and forth through the sock and leg (Fig. 7).

✪ Tuck each sock into the uncinched ankle yo-yo. Cinch the yo-yo over the sock and slipstitch in place.

Shoes

⊗ Put an extra-large yo-yo over each sock for the shoes. Fold over and attach to the bottom of the sock on each foot with a slip-stitch.

Arms

⊗ Put an extra-large yo-yo on the doll's right arm and pull up to the shoulder. Repeat on the left arm. Tuck the yo-yos in between the first neck yo-yo and the first chest yo-yo.

⊗ Slipstitch the yo-yos on the left and right arms together, crossing through the chest. Then slipstitch the arm yo-yos to the chest yo-yo (Fig. 8).

⊗ Put additional extra-large yo-yos on each arm, ending with an uncinched wrist yo-yo.

⊗ Attach the hands to the arms using a slipstitch, inserting the needle back and forth (Fig. 9).

⊗ Pull the wrist yo-yos over the hands and cinch shut. Tack the wrist yo-yos to the hands (Fig. 10).

Hair

⊗ The hair for each doll starts out the same way. Cut very small slits in the head about a ¼" apart all around the hairline and throughout the crown, sides, and back of the head. (I discovered you save a lot of wear and tear on your fingers by doing this. It is hard to pull a doll needle with yarn in it through the doll's head.)

⊗ Thread 24" lengths of the yarn specified in the pattern. Insert the needle in one slit and out another. Tie a knot in the yarn and cut both ends of the yarn a little longer than the final length you want. (Refer to the photo of the doll or choose your own length.)

⊗ Continue adding strands of yarn throughout the top, sides, and back of the head. Make the hair for the bangs shorter.

⊗ Smooth down all the hair and trim to the final length you want. Fluff it like you would your own hair.

Fig. 8

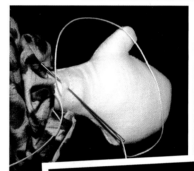

Fig. 9

Fig. 10

Hint: If the yarn you choose has a thread running through it and you want to make the hair look fluffier, carefully pull the thread out before tying the knot in the yarn. I left the thread in on Auntie Em's hair but removed it from the yarn on Victoria.

ЧO-ЧO DOLLS & DOLL QUILTS

Mary Ellen and
Yo-Yos All in a Row

MARY ELLEN

Materials and Supplies

Clover yo-yo makers (small, large, extra large, and jumbo)

Basic yo-yo doll supplies (page 11)

⅔ yard each of 4 coordinating prints (2⅔ yards total)

Note: If you are going to make Mary Ellen's yo-yo quilt, you will need an additional ¾ yard of each of the fabrics.

¼ yard ivory (for the body)

Scrap of white (for the socks)

Scrap of black (for the shoes)

Yellow yarn

¼ yard HeatnBond fusible interfacing

1 – ⁷⁄₁₆" half ball cover button

2 – ½" white buttons (for the eyes)

2 – small blue buttons (for the eyes)

2 – 2mm rhinestones (for the eyes)

2 small pink heart-shaped buttons

6mm pearls (cream)

4mm pearls (cream)

1 pearl flower button

Making the Doll
Body

✖ Trace Mary Ellen's pattern (page 74). Make her head, hands, body, and face according to the general instructions (pages 12–13).

Yo-Yos

Fabric	# of squares	Size of squares	Yo-Yo Maker to Use	Placement
assorted prints	11	8½" x 8½"	Jumbo (blue)	torso
	37	5½" x 5½"	Extra large (yellow)	arms (5 each)
				legs (13 each)
				neck (1)
	3	4½" x 4½"	Large (orange)	arms (1 each)
				neck (1)
	2	3" x 3"	Small (green)	wrists
white	2	5½" x 5½"	Extra large (yellow)	socks
black	2	5½" x 5½"	Extra large (yellow)	shoes

Cutting Instructions

For the jumbo yo-yos:

- ✺ Cut an 8½" strip from each of the 4 coordinating prints.
- ✺ Cut 3 – 8½" x 8½"" squares from 3 of the fabrics.
- ✺ Cut 2 – 8½" x 8½" squares from the fourth fabric.

For the extra-large yo-yos:

- ✺ Cut 2 – 5½" strips from each of the 4 coordinating prints.
- ✺ Cut a mix of 37 – 5½" x 5½" squares.

For the large yo-yos:

- ✺ Cut 3 – 4½" x 4½" squares from one of the coordinating fabrics.

For the small yo-yos:

- ✺ Cut 2 – 3" x 3" squares from the same fabric as the large yo-yos.

For the socks:

- ✺ Cut 2 white 5½" x 5½" squares.

For the shoes:

- ✺ Cut 2 black 5½" x 5½" squares.
- ✺ Cut 11 – 2" x 2" squares and 44 – 1½" x 1½" squares of HeatnBond.

✺ Iron the larger squares of interfacing onto the center of the wrong side of the jumbo yo-yo fabric squares and the smaller squares onto the other yo-yo fabric squares, following the manufacturer's instructions. *The socks and shoes yo-yos don't need to be fused.*

✺ Cut a star-shaped opening in the center of the fused fabric squares (page 15), then peel off the paper.

✺ Insert the fabric squares into the appropriate size yo-yo makers and follow the manufacturer's instructions. Leave an 8" tail of thread on 1 extra-large and 1 large neck yo-yo; the 2 extra-large ankle yo-yos; the 2 small wrist yo-yos; and the shoes and socks yo-yos. They'll be cinched after they're added to the doll. All the other yo-yos can be cinched shut leaving about a half-inch opening.

✺ Dress Mary Ellen with the yo-yos as described in Yo-Yos Dress the Doll (pages 15–17). Refer to the yo-yos table (page 19) for placement of the yo-yos.

Finishing Touches

Shoes

✺ Make a strap for the shoes with ¼" bias tape.

✺ Position the strap over the sock and slipstitch to both top edges of the shoe. Sew a heart-shaped pink button at the outside end of the strap.

Hair

✺ Add the hair (page 17) and trim to about 5" long.

Necklace

✺ String 35–40 6mm pearls on about 8" of stretchy jewelry cord. Tie it with a square knot. Clip the ends and put over Mary Ellen's neck. Wrap the necklace around her neck twice.

Bracelet

✺ String 12 – 6mm pearls on about 5" of stretchy jewelry cord. Tie with a square knot. Clip the ends and put on Mary Ellen's wrist.

Make-Up

✺ Apply pink chalk to her cheeks with a chalk puff or a Q-tip.

YO-YOS ALL IN A ROW

9" x 9", made by the author

Traditionally yo-yos are stitched together separately with very small stitches to make a quilt. Normal wear and tear breaks down the stitches after awhile and they have to be redone. These yo-yo quilts need a lot of upkeep.

Mary Ellen loves traditional things, but used a new approach to put her quilt together. It would take a lot of wear and tear for this little quilt to come apart! This same method could be used on a full sized yo-yo quilt as well!

Materials and Supplies

Clover (small) yo-yo maker
¼" bias tape maker
⅓ yard main print (print 1: for outer and centermost yo-yos)
¼ yard each of 3 coordinating print fabrics
⅛ yard HeatnBond fusible interfacing
Quilt label (page 78)
Fabric glue

Yo-Yos

Fabric	# of squares	Size of squares	Yo-Yo Maker to Use	Placement
print 1	33	3" x 3"	Small (green)	5th (outer) round (32) center (1)
print 2	24	3" x 3"	Small (green)	4th round
print 3	16	3" x 3"	Small (green)	3rd round
print 4	8	3" x 3"	Small (green)	2nd round

Cutting Instructions

✺ Cut 3 – 3" strips of print 1 into 33 – 3" x 3" squares.

✺ Cut 2 – 3" strips of print 2 into 24 – 3" x 3" squares.

✺ Cut 2 – 3" strips of print 3 into 16 – 3" x 3" squares.

✺ Cut 1 – 3" strip of print 4 into 8 – 3" x 3" squares.

✺ Cut 81 – ¾" x ¾" squares of HeatnBond. *Fuse to the center of the wrong side of the yo-yo squares.*

Cut 4 – ¼" slits

Fig. 1

Making Bias Strips

✺ Cut 18 – ½" x 12" bias strips from any or all of the print fabrics. Fold and press using a ¼" bias tape maker and follow the manufacturer's instructions.

Making the Quilt

✺ Make 81 yo-yos using the small yo-yo maker and follow the manufacturer's instructions.

✺ Cut 4 – ¼" slits in the back of each yo-yo as shown (Fig. 1).

✺ Lay out the yo-yos on a table, cut side up, in the arrangement shown (Fig. 2).

✺ Lace the bias strips through each horizontal row of yo-yos. Then lace the remaining bias strips through the vertical rows. When all the yo-yos are laced and in position, lightly iron from the bias-strip side. The interfacing will adhere to the bias strip (Fig. 3, page 23).

✺ Tuck in the ends of the strips and secure with stitching or fabric glue.

✺ Sew your label on the bottom left-hand corner of the back.

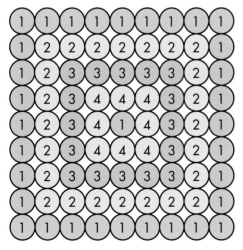

Fig. 2

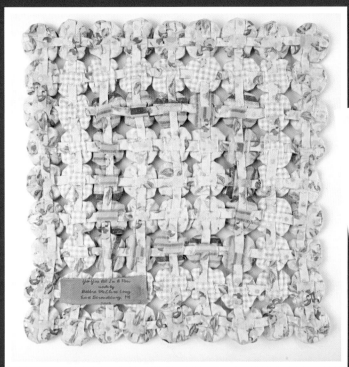

Fig. 3

Mary Ellen and Victoria with their quilts.

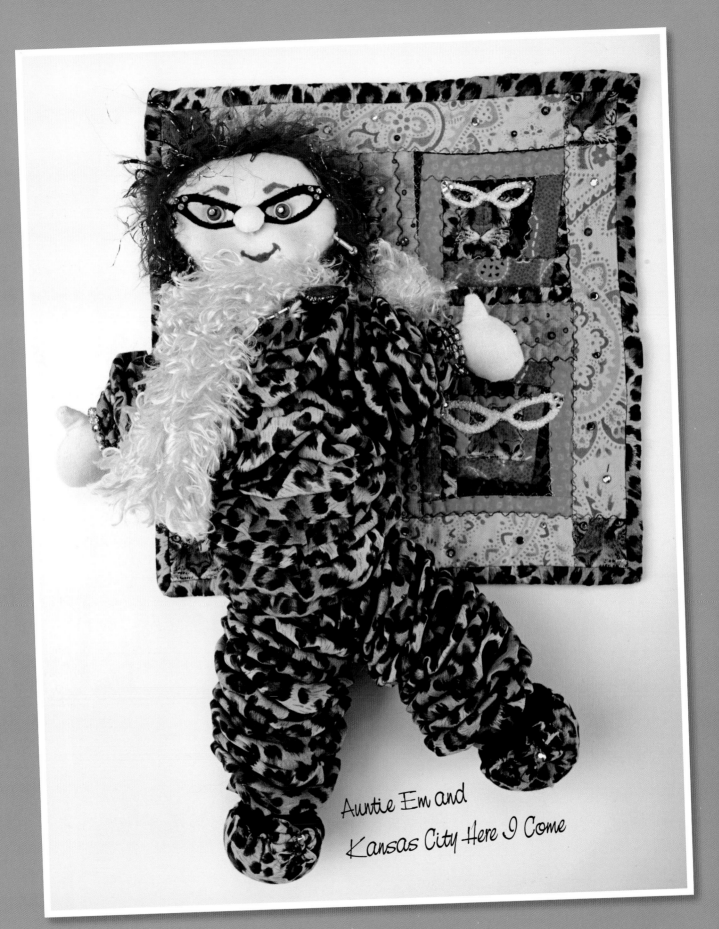

Auntie Em and
Kansas City Here I Come

AUNTIE EM

Materials and Supplies

Clover yo-yo makers (small, large, extra large, and jumbo)

Basic yo-yo doll supplies (page 11)

1⅞ yards leopard print (for the yo-yos)

¼ yard ivory (for the body)

Scrap of black (for the glasses and socks)

Red yarn (I used Moda Dea® Frivolous yarn, Berry Nice 9912.)

¼ yard HeatnBond fusible interfacing

1 – ⁷⁄₁₆" half ball cover button

2 – ¼" purple buttons (for the eyes)

6 crystal 2mm rhinestones

2 aurora borealis 2mm rhinestones (for the eyes)

2 aurora borealis 4mm rhinestones

Blue and green glass seed beads

¼" silver-plated glass bugle beads

4mm faceted round silver mirror beads (optional)

¼" glass silver-plated bugle beads

1 heart-shaped charm for necklace (optional)

½" silver charm with rhinestone center (optional for bracelet)

Lime green 3" polyester craft trim

Baby blue scrapbooking chalk

Fig. 1

Making the Doll
Body

❂ Trace Auntie Em's pattern (page 74). Make her head, hands, body, and face according to the general instructions (pages 12–13).

❂ Fuse her glasses onto her head before attaching her nose.

Making Auntie Em's Glasses

❂ Trace glasses (page 77) on the smooth side of the HeatnBond. Cut out 1" beyond the drawn lines and fuse to back side of the black fabric. Use sharp scissors with small blades to cut out the lenses, then cut around the outside of the frames (Fig. 1).

❂ Cut 2 – ⅛" x ½" strips of fabric from leftover glasses fabric that has HeatnBond on the back for the arms of the glasses.

❂ Fuse the glasses frames above the hole where the nose will go.

❂ Add 3 crystal 2mm rhinestones on each point of the glasses.

Aurora borealis 2mm rhinestones will be added to each eye to give her twinkling eyes as shown in the picture.

HINT: Cut the inside of the glasses out first, and then carefully cut out the outside.

Yo-Yos

Fabric	# of squares	Size of squares	Yo-Yo Maker to Use	Placement
leopard print	11	8½" x 8½"	Jumbo (blue)	torso
	39	5½" x 5½"	Extra large (yellow)	arms (6 each)
				legs (12 each)
				neck (1)
				shoes (2)
	5	4½" x 4½"	Large (orange)	wrists (2)
				ankles (2)
				neck (1)
	4	3" x 3"	Small (green)	bows for shoes (2)
				wrists (2)
black	2	5½" x 5½"	Extra large (yellow)	socks

Cutting Instructions

For the jumbo yo-yos:
✪ Cut 3 – 8½" strips of leopard print.

✪ Cut 11 – 8½" x 8½" squares.

For the extra-large yo-yos:
✪ Cut 6 – 5½" strips of leopard print.

✪ Cut 39 – 5½" x 5½" squares.

For the large yo-yos:
✪ Cut 1 – 4½" strip of leopard print.

✪ Cut 5 – 4½" x 4½" squares.

For the small yo-yos:
✪ Cut 4– 3" x 3" squares of leopard print.

For the socks:
✪ Cut 2 – 5½" x 5½" black squares.

✪ Cut 11 – 2" x 2" squares and 44 – 1½" x 1½" squares of HeatnBond.

✪ Iron the larger squares of interfacing onto the center of the wrong side of the jumbo yo-yo fabric squares and the smaller squares onto the other yo-yo fabric squares, following the manufacturer's instructions. *The yo-yos for the socks, shoes, and bows on the shoes don't need to be fused.*

✪ Cut a star-shaped opening in the center of the fused fabric squares (page 15), then peel off the paper.

✪ Insert the fabric squares into the appropriate size yo-yo makers and follow the manufacturer's instructions. Leave an 8" tail of thread on 1 extra-large and 1 large neck yo-yo; the 2 large ankle yo-yos; the 2 small wrist yo-yos; and the 2 sock and 2 shoe yo-yos. They'll be cinched after they're added to the doll. All the other yo-yos can be cinched shut leaving about a half-inch opening.

✪ Dress Auntie Em with the yo-yos as described in Yo-Yos Dress the Doll (pages 15–17). Refer to the yo-yo table (this page) for placement of the yo-yos.

Finishing Touches

Hair

⊗ Add the hair (page 17) and trim to 1" long.

Bracelets

⊗ String blue and green seed beads on stretchy jewelry cord. Put a ½" silver medallion with rhinestone center in the center of the beads. Tie the ends with a square knot and slip over the wrist.

⊗ To make the other bracelet, string silver beads on stretchy jewelry cord, tie a square knot, and slip over the other wrist.

Earrings

⊗ String a silver bugle bead, a round silver bead, and another silver bugle bead on stretchy jewelry cord. Then make a loop. Attach the loop to the head where the bottom of the ear would be.

Boa

⊗ Cut a 3" x 12" strip of lime green polyester craft trim. Sew right sides together on 3 sides. Turn and slipstitch closed. Tie around Auntie Em's neck.

Make-Up

⊗ Apply pink chalk to her cheeks and blue chalk above her eyes with a chalk puff or a Q-tip. Use a different applicator for each color.

KANSAS CITY HERE I COME

9½" x 9½", made by the author

Auntie Em's quilt is as eccentric as she is. It sparkles with multicolored rhinestones. Tigers look out from behind white sunglasses. Yes, that's right, tigers. It doesn't make a bit of difference that the quilt is bordered with leopard fabric, or that the yo-yos Auntie Em is wearing have the leopard's spots. She likes all the big cats no matter which fur they are in.

The crazy Log Cabin quilt blocks are as individual as you and I and Auntie Em are. They give you a chance to let go, be wild and crazy, and experiment with your own distinctive style.

Materials and Supplies

⅓ yard animal print fabric
(I used Robert Kaufman Screen Print D #5506 Portraits of the Wild.)
Scraps of 4 assorted coordinating prints (for crazy Log Cabin blocks)
Scrap of white for the glasses
Scrap of green print (for sashing)
Fat eighth light print (for borders)
Scraps of HeatnBond fusible interfacing
11½" x 11½" square batting
Multicolored 2mm rhinestones
Multicolored 4mm rhinestones
Quilt label (page 78)

Cutting Instructions

From the animal print:

- Fussy cut 8 – 1½" x 1½" tiger face squares (for block centers and cornerstones).
- Cut 1 –11½" x 11½" square (for backing).
- Cut 1 – 2½" x 40" strip (for binding).

From the 4 assorted prints:

- Cut 12 each 1" x 3½" strips (48 total).

From the green print:

- Cut 1 – 1½" x 7½" sashing strip.
- Cut 2 – 1½" x 3½" sashing strips.

From the light print border print:

- Cut 4 – 1½" x 7½" strips.

Making the Quilt

The 4 blocks are made almost like a traditional Log Cabin block. Use the quilt photograph as a guide and have fun!

- Sew a 1½" x 3" strip to one side of a fussy cut square at a slight angle. Trim the ends even with the square (Fig. 1).

- Add a second 1½" x 3" strip of the same fabric to an adjacent side and trim as before (Fig. 2).

- Add 2 matching 1½" x 3" strips to the remaining 2 sides and trim at an angle. Trim the sides of the square at an angle.

- Add 2 more rounds of 1½" x 3" strips, trimming as you go.

- Square up the block to measure 3½" x 3½" (Fig. 3).

- Repeat these steps for the other 3 blocks.

- Lay out the blocks and sashing strips as shown in figure 4, page 30.

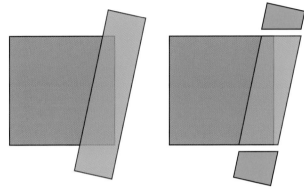

Fig. 1

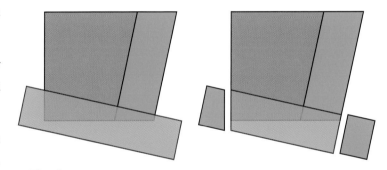

Fig. 2

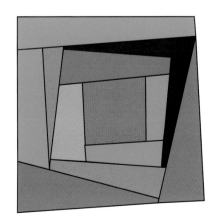

Fig. 3

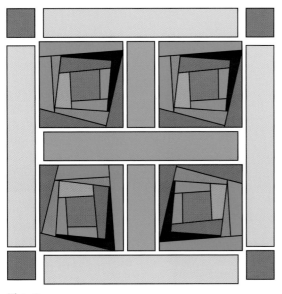

Fig. 4

❂ Join the components into rows and sew the rows together.

❂ Add 2 border strips to opposite sides of the quilt top.

❂ Add the 1½" cornerstones to both ends of the remaining border strips and add to the other 2 sides of the quilt top.

❂ Square up to measure 9½" x 9½".

Finishing

❂ Trace 4 pairs of glasses (page 77) on the smooth side of HeatnBond.

❂ Fuse the interfacing to the back side of a scrap of white fabric. Cut out the inside of the frames, then the outside, using sharp scissors with small blades.

❂ Fuse a pair of glasses on each of the four tigers in the center of the blocks. Buttonhole stitch around the inside and outside edges with white thread. Add 3 crystal 2mm rhinestones on the outside points of the glasses.

❂ Layer the top with the batting and backing and quilt along all the seam lines with a bright variegated thread using a wavy decorative stitch. Stitch a double row on the sashing.

❂ Trim the backing and batting even with the quilt top. Fold the binding strip in half lengthwise and press.

❂ Sew the binding to the quilt top with a ¼" seam. Fold to the back and hand stitch in place.

❂ Add colored 2mm and 3mm rhinestones throughout the top of the quilt.

❂ Sew your label on the bottom left hand corner of the back.

Victoria and
Victoria's Quilt

VICTORIA

Materials and Supplies

Clover yo-yo makers (small, large, extra large, and jumbo)

Basic yo-yo doll supplies (page 11)

1½ yards blue velvet

¼ yard lace fabric

¼ yard ivory

Scrap of white satin (for socks)

Scrap of black velvet (for shoes)

Light brown yarn (I used Lion Brand® Homespun® Yarn in Barley.)

¼ yard HeatnBond fusible interfacing

4 pink ribbon roses

1 – ⁷⁄₁₆" half ball cover button (for the nose)

2 – ½" white buttons (for the eyes)

2 – small blue buttons (for the eyes)

4 – small black buttons (for the shoes)

6 – 2mm rhinestones (for eyes and shoes)

1 package 4mm clear Swarovski® crystal bicone beads

Making the Doll
Body

⊗ Trace Victoria's pattern (page 74). Make her head, hands, body, and face according to the general instructions (pages 12–13).

Yo-Yos

Fabric	# of squares	Size of squares	Yo-Yo Maker to Use	Placement
blue velvet	8	8½" x 8½"	Jumbo (blue)	torso
	28	5½" x 5½"	Extra large (yellow)	arms (4 each)
				legs (10 each)
	2	4½" x 4½"	Large (orange)	arms (1 each)
lace fabric	1	5½" x 5½"	Extra large (yellow)	neck
	3	4½" x 4½"	Large (orange)	arms (1 each)
				neck (1)
	2	3" x 3"	Small (green)	wrists
white satin	2	5½" x 5½"	Extra large (yellow)	socks
black velvet	2	5½" x 5½"	Extra large (yellow)	shoes

Cutting Instructions

For the jumbo yo-yos:
- ❊ Cut 2 – 8½" strips of blue velvet.
- ❊ Cut into 8 – 8½" x 8½" squares.

For the extra-large yo-yos:
- ❊ Cut 4 – 5½" strips of blue velvet.
- ❊ Cut into 28 – 5½" x 5½" squares.
- ❊ Cut 1 – 5½" x 5½" square of lace fabric.

For the large yo-yos:
- ❊ Cut 2 – 4½" x 4½" blue velvet squares.
- ❊ Cut 3 – 4½" x 4½" lace fabric squares.

For the small yo-yos:
- ❊ Cut 2 – 3" x 3" lace fabric squares.

For the socks:
- ❊ Cut 2 white satin 5½" x 5½" squares.

For the shoes:
- ❊ Cut 2 black velvet 5½" x 5½" squares.

- ❊ Cut 8 – 2" x 2" squares and 32 – 1½" x 1½" squares of HeatnBond.

❊ Iron the larger squares of interfacing onto the center of the wrong side of the jumbo yo-yo fabric squares and the smaller squares onto the other yo-yo fabric squares, following the manufacturer's instructions. *The yo-yos for the socks, shoes, and bows on the shoes don't need to be fused.*

❊ Cut a star-shaped opening in the center of the fused fabric squares (page 15), then peel off the paper.

❊ Insert the fabric squares into the appropriate size yo-yo makers and follow the manufacturer's instructions. Remember to leave an 8" tail of thread on 1 extra-large and 1 large neck yo-yo; the 2 large ankle yo-yos; the 2 small wrist yo-yos; and the 2 sock and 2 shoe yo-yos. They'll be cinched after they're added to the doll. All the other yo-yos can be cinched shut leaving about a half-inch opening.

❊ Dress Victoria with the yo-yos as described in Yo-Yos Dress the Doll (pages 15–17). Refer to the yo-yo table (page 32) for placement of the yo-yos.

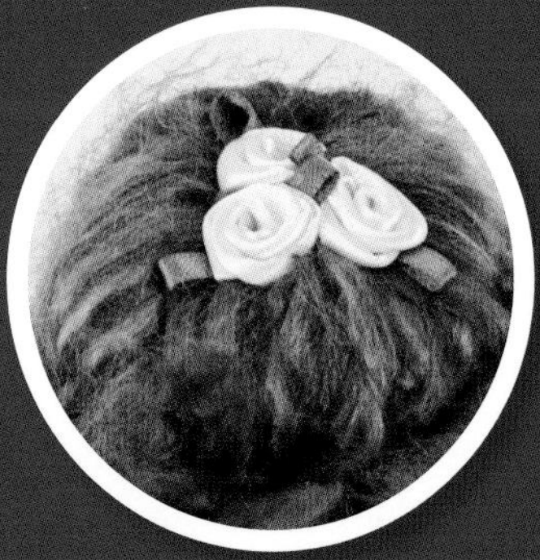

Finishing Touches

Hair

Add the hair (page 17), trim bangs, and cut the rest of the hair so it reaches to about the mid-point of Victoria's back.

Pull the upper sides of her hair to the back of her head and form a small bun. Slipstitch it together they way you would apply hairpins in real hair.

Slipstitch 3 pink ribbon roses in the bun. Then smooth all the hair down and trim to the final length you want. Fluff it like you would your own hair.

Necklace

String about 20 crystal beads on 10" of stretchy jewelry cord. Tie with a square knot. Clip the ends and put over Victoria's neck.

Sew a pink ribbon rose onto the lace yo-yo at the neck.

Shoes

Sew 2 black buttons to the front of the shoes. Add a 2mm rhinestone to the center of each button.

Make-Up

Apply pink chalk to her cheeks with a chalk puff or a Q-tip. Use a different applicator for each color.

VICTORIA'S QUILT

6½" x 6¾" plus a 1½" fringe, made by the author

VICTORIA'S QUILT is made of scraps of velvet and cotton fabrics with ribbon, beads, and lace. Like any crazy quilt, you can add just about anything you want! The quilt is fused and sewn together before you know it. Use the pattern as a guide. If you want to make the shapes a little differently go right ahead. Each crazy quilt is always just a little different. The "squares" are sewn together with gold metallic thread using fancy sewing machine stitches to give it that hand-sewn embroidered look.

Materials and Supplies

Fabrics, ribbon, beads, and thread of your choice can be substituted for the ones listed. See what you have on hand before you get started.

Scraps of assorted velvets, lace, and satin
8" x 8" square of muslin
9" x 9" square of backing (I used a printed satin.)
¼ yard HeatnBond fusible interfacing
1 pink ribbon rose
Dark blue, light blue, white, and gold seed beads
Green velvet ribbon
1 – 4mm gold bead
1 – 4mm Swarovski crystal bead
¾ yard 2" light blue fringe
Masking tape
Quilt label (page 78)

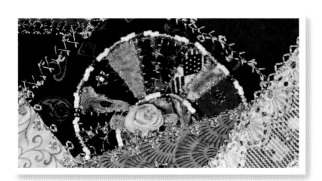

Making the Quilt
Preparing the Fabric Pieces

✖ Trace each individual shape from the quilt pattern (page 77) onto the shiny side of the light HeatnBond. Leave at least a ½" between each piece. Trace 2 of piece #21.

✖ Cut out all the interfacing pieces, leaving ¼" around each piece.

✖ Iron the pieces to the wrong side of fabrics of your choice. Fuse the second piece #21 onto the lace fabric.

✖ Cut out each piece on the line. Loosen a corner of the interfacing and remove the paper.

✖ Embroider Victoria's name on piece #10 using your sewing machine or by hand.

Quilt Assembly

✖ Draw a 6½" x 6½" square onto an 8" x 8" square of muslin. Referring to the assembly diagram (Fig. 1), place each piece onto the muslin, placing the lace over piece #21.

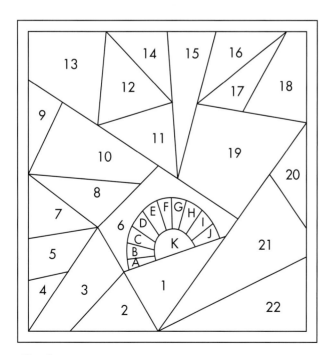

Fig. 1.

✖ Fuse the pieces in place as you position each one or wait until they're all arranged before fusing them.

✖ Machine appliqué each piece using decorative stitches of your choice and gold metallic thread.

✖ Make 2 strings of 4 light blue, 4 white, and 4 dark blue seed beads on upholstery thread, continuing the pattern until the strings are long enough to go around the outer and inner fan edges. Tack down every fourth bead.

✖ Add decorative lace, ribbon roses, and additional beads.

Adding the Fringe

✖ Lay the quilt right-side up on a flat surface.

✖ Lay the fringe around the perimeter of the quilt with the fringe facing in. (Edging will overhang the quilt so that it will not show when you sew and turn the quilt.)

✖ Tape down the fringe with masking tape.

✖ Lay the backing fabric right-side down on top of the quilt and fringe. Pin them together.

✖ Carefully sew around the quilt with a ¼" seam, leaving a 3" opening, backstitching at the beginning and end. Remove the pins as you go and be careful not to sew over any of the beads.

✖ Turn the quilt right-side out, making sure the fringe isn't caught in the seam. With the eraser on a pencil, ease the corners into a slightly rounded shape. Hand stitch the opening closed.

✖ Sew your label on the back in the bottom left corner.

Carolyn and
Carolyn's Garden

CAROLYN

Materials and Supplies

Clover yo-yo makers (small, large,
   extra large, and jumbo)
Basic yo-yo doll supplies (page 11)
1¾ yards dark blue print
⅜ yard light print
¼ yard brown fabric (for the body)
Scrap of blue (for the shoes)
Scrap of aqua (for the socks)
Black yarn (I used Lion Brand Homespun.)
¼ yard HeatnBond fusible interfacing
1 – $\frac{7}{16}$" half ball cover button (for the nose)
2 – ½" white buttons (for the eyes)
2 – small brown buttons (for the eyes)
2 – 2mm rhinestones (for the eyes)
Assorted 6mm blue beads

Making the Doll
Body

Trace Carolyn's pattern (page 74). Make her
head, hands, body, and face according to the general instructions (pages 12–13).

Yo-Yos

Fabric	# of squares	Size of squares	Yo-Yo Maker to Use	Placement
dark blue print	10	8½" x 8½"	Jumbo (blue)	torso
	38	5½" x 5½"	Extra large (yellow)	arms (6 each)
				legs (13 each)
light print	1	5½" x 5½"	Extra large (yellow)	neck
	3	4½" x 4½"	Large (orange)	neck (1)
				wrists (1 each)
	4	3" x 3"	Small (green)	wrists (1 each)
				bows on shoes (1 each)
solid aqua	2	5½" x 5½"	Extra large (yellow)	socks
solid blue	2	5½" x 5½"	Extra large (yellow)	shoes

Cutting Instructions

For the jumbo yo-yos:
- ❋ Cut 3 – 8½" strips from the dark blue print.
- ❋ Cut 10 – 8½" x 8½" squares.

For the extra-large yo-yos:
- ❋ Cut 6 – 5½" strips from the dark blue print.
- ❋ Cut 38 – 5½" x 5½" squares.
- ❋ Cut 1 – 5½" x 5½" square from the light print.

For the large yo-yos:
- ❋ Cut 1 – 4½" strip of light print.
- ❋ Cut 3 – 4½" x 4½" squares.

For the small yo-yos:
- ❋ Cut 1 – 3" strip of light print.
- ❋ Cut 4 – 3" x 3" squares.

For the socks:
- ❋ Cut 2 solid aqua 5½" x 5½" squares.

For the shoes:
- ❋ Cut 2 solid blue 5½" x 5½" squares.
- ❋ Cut 10 – 2" x 2" squares and 44 – 1½" x 1½" squares of HeatnBond.

❋ Iron the larger squares of interfacing onto the center of the wrong side of the jumbo yo-yo fabric squares and the smaller squares onto the other yo-yo fabric squares, following the manufacturer's instructions. *The socks, shoes, and bows yo-yos don't need to be fused.*

❋ Cut a star-shaped opening in the center of the fused fabric squares (page 15), then peel off the paper.

❋ Insert the fabric squares into the appropriate size yo-yo makers and follow the manufacturer's instructions. Leave an 8" tail of thread on 1 extra-large and 1 large neck yo-yo; the 2 extra large ankle yo-yos; the 2 small wrist yo-yos; and the shoes and socks yo-yos. They'll be cinched after they're added to the doll. All the other yo-yos can be cinched shut leaving about a half-inch opening.

❋ Dress Carolyn with the yo-yos as described in Yo-Yos Dress the Doll (pages 15–17). Refer to the yo-yo table (page 38) for placement of the yo-yos.

Finishing Touches
Hair
❋ Add the hair (page 17) and trim to 5" long.

Necklace
❋ String 20 – 6mm assorted blue beads on 12" of stretchy jewelry cord. Tie with a square knot. Clip the ends and put over Carolyn's neck.

Bracelet
❋ String 16 – 6mm assorted blue beads on 5" of stretchy jewelry cord. Tie with a square knot. Clip the ends and put on Carolyn's wrist.

Shoes
❋ Fasten the small light print yo-yos to the front of the shoes, pulling the thread around them to create a bow shape.

Make-Up
❋ Apply red chalk to her cheeks with a chalk puff or a Q-tip.

CAROLYN'S GARDEN

9½" x 9½", made by the author

CAROLYN'S GARDEN is made with some of the blue fabric that she is so fond of. She likes to sit with it on her lap on cool spring nights while she admires the new flowers coming up in her garden.

Materials and Supplies

Scraps of 7 assorted prints (for blocks and
flowers; one large enough for binding)
⅛ yard HeatnBond fusible interfacing
Fat eighth of rose (for the borders)
10½" x 10½" backing
10½" x 10½" batting
Quilt label (page 78)

Cutting Instructions

⊗ Cut 2–3 – 2½" x 2½" squares from the 7 assorted prints (16 total) (for the blocks).

⊗ Cut 2–3 – 1½" x 1½" squares from the 7 assorted prints (16 total) (for the flower petals).

⊗ Cut 2–3 – ½" x ½" squares from the 7 assorted prints (16 total) (for the flower centers).

⊗ Cut 4 – 1" x 8½" rose strips (for the borders).

⊗ Cut 4 – 1" x 1" squares (for the cornerstones).

⊗ Cut enough 2½" wide strips for a length of 42" (for the binding).

Making the Quilt

Granny's Flowers

Trace 16 flower petal patterns and 16 flower center patterns (page 74) onto the paper side of HeatnBond, leaving at least ¼" between the motifs. Cut out ⅛" beyond the drawn line.

Fuse the prepared flower petals to the wrong side of the 1½" x 1½" squares. Cut out on the line. Loosen a corner of the interfacing and remove the paper.

Fuse the prepared flower centers to the wrong side of the ½" x ½" squares. Cut out on the line. Loosen a corner of the interfacing and remove the paper.

Quilt Assembly

Lay out the 16 – 2½" x 2½" squares in a 4 x 4 arrangement, making sure matching fabric squares are not next to each other.

Join the squares into rows, pressing the seams in alternate rows in opposite directions.

Sew the rows together.

Position the prepared petals on the blocks to make sure all the petals contrast with the block fabrics. Fuse the petals to the center of the 16 blocks.

Position the prepared centers on the petals to ensure all the centers contrast with the petals. Fuse the flower centers to the petals.

Pin the quilt top in the center of the 10½" x 10½" square of batting.

With contrasting thread, define the 6 individual flower petals with a buttonhole stitch. This will also define the centers and make it look like you sewed each petal on individually! (The buttonhole stitch can be done by hand or you can use a straight or zigzag stitch on your sewing machine.)

Add diagonal quilting through the centers of the blocks, stopping at each flower and continuing on its opposite side.

Border

Sew 1" x 8½" border strips to opposite sides of the top. Stitch through the batting. Press away from the center.

Sew the 1" x 1" cornerstones to opposite ends of the remaining two 1" x 8½" border strips. Sew to opposite sides of the top. Press away from the center.

Finishing

Iron the quilt top and batting to the 10½"x 10½" square of backing. Trim the batting and backing even with the quilt top.

Join the binding strips end-to-end. Fold under one long side ¼" and press. Sew the unfolded edge of the binding to the quilt with a ¼" seam. Fold the binding to the back. Add a serpentine decorative stitch along both sides of the border, which will secure the folded edge of the binding on the back.

Sew your label on the back in the bottom left corner (Fig. 1).

Fig. 1

Sam and
Bear Country

SAM

Materials and Supplies

    Clover yo-yo makers (small, large, extra large, and jumbo)
    Basic yo-yo doll supplies (page 11)
    1⅜ yards red plaid
    1⅝ yards denim blue
    ¼ yard ivory (for the body)
    Scrap of red (for the socks)
    Scrap of brown suede (for the shoes)
    Light brown yarn (I used Lion Brand Homespun Yarn in Barley.)
    ¼ yard HeatnBond fusible interfacing
    1 – 9/16" half ball covered button (for the nose)
    2 – ½" white buttons (for the eyes)
    2 – small brown buttons (for the eyes)
    2 – 2mm rhinestones (for the eyes)
    8 brown rivets (for the shoe laces)
    Brown embroidery or craft thread

Making the Doll
Body

    ⊗ Trace Sam's pattern (page 75). Make his head, hands, body, and face according to the general instructions (pages 12–13).

Yo-Yos

Fabric	# of squares	Size of squares	Yo-Yo Maker to Use	Placement
red plaid	9	8½" x 8½"	Jumbo (blue)	torso
	15	5½" x 5½"	Extra large (yellow)	arms (6 each)
				neck (3)
	4	4½" x 4½"	Large (orange)	wrists (2 each)
denim blue	5	8½" x 8½"	Jumbo (blue)	torso
	44	5½" x 5½"	Extra large (yellow)	legs (22 each)
red	2	5½" x 5½"	Extra large (yellow)	socks
brown suede	2	5½" x 5½"	Extra large (yellow)	shoes

Cutting Instructions

For the jumbo yo-yos:
- ✪ Cut 3 – 8½" strips of red plaid.
- ✪ Cut 9 – 8½" x 8½" squares.
- ✪ Cut 2 – 8½" strips of denim blue.
- ✪ Cut 5 – 8½" x 8½" squares.

For the extra-large yo-yos:
- ✪ Cut 3 – 5½" strips of red plaid.
- ✪ Cut 15 – 5½" x 5½" squares.
- ✪ Cut 7 – 5½" strips of denim blue.
- ✪ Cut 44 – 5½" x 5½" squares.

For the large yo-yos:
- ✪ Cut 1 – 4½" strip of red plaid.
- ✪ Cut 4 – 4½" x 4½" squares.

For the socks:
- ✪ Cut 2 red 5½" x 5½" squares.

For the shoes:
- ✪ Cut 2 brown suede 5½" x 5½" squares.

- ✪ Cut 14 – 2" x 2" squares and 63 – 1½" x 1½" squares of HeatnBond.

✪ Iron the larger squares of interfacing onto the center of the wrong side of the jumbo yo-yo fabric squares and the smaller squares onto the other yo-yo fabric squares, following the manufacturer's instructions. *The socks and shoes yo-yos don't need to be fused.*

✪ Cut a star-shaped opening in the center of the fused fabric squares (page 15), then peel off the paper.

✪ Insert the fabric squares into the appropriate size yo-yo makers and follow the manufacturer's instructions. Leave an 8" tail of thread on 1 extra-large red plaid neck yo-yo; the 2 extra-large denim blue yo-yos for the ankles; the 2 large red plaid yo-yos for the wrists; and the shoes and socks yo-yos. They'll be cinched after they're added to the doll. All the other yo-yos can be cinched shut leaving about a half-inch opening.

✪ Dress Sam with the yo-yos as described in Yo-Yos Dress the Doll (pages 15–17). Refer to the table (page 43) for placement of the yo-yos.

Finishing Touches
Hair

✪ Add the hair (page 17) and trim ¾" long in the front and ½" in the back.

Shoes

✪ Insert 4 rivets in the front of each shoe following manufacturer's instructions.

✪ Lace brown embroidery or craft thread though the holes leaving about 5" tails.

✪ Put the shoes over each sock. Attach with a slipstitch and tie the laces. Double knot them and trim the tails to the length you want.

Face

✪ Apply pink chalk sparingly to his cheeks with a chalk puff or a Q-tip.

BEAR COUNTRY
10½" x 10½", made by the author

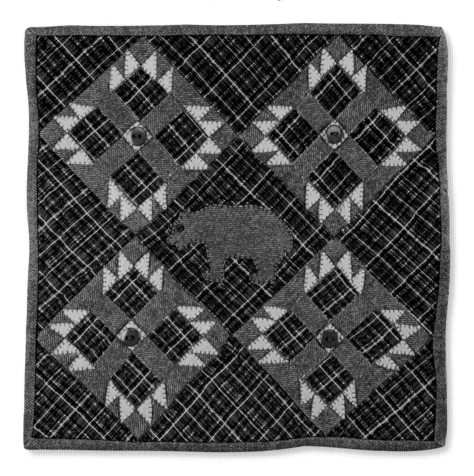

Squares sewn on point and appliquéd triangles give this little quilt its Bear Paw look. The center bear made of look-alike blue denim fabric adds to the rustic look of this quilt that Sam enjoys so much. It is fun and a lot easier to make than it looks.

Materials and Supplies

Fat quarter dark red plaid fabric
Fat eighth denim-colored blue cotton
10" x 10" tan felt (for the bear claw triangles)
⅛ yard HeatnBond Light
12" x 12" backing
12" x 12" cotton batting
4 – ½" red buttons (for the blocks)
1 – ¼" black button (for the bear's eye)
Quilt label (page 78)

Cutting Instructions

From the red plaid:

- ❌ Cut 1 – 4" x 4" square.
- ❌ Cut 3 – 4½" x 4½" squares.
- ❌ Cut 2 in half once on the diagonal (for the side setting triangles).
- ❌ Cut 1 in half twice on the diagonal (for the corner setting triangles).
- ❌ Cut 4 – 3" x 3" squares (for the blue block centers).

From the denim-colored blue:

- ❌ Cut a 1" x 20" strip of HeatnBond and fuse to the back of the blue fabric.
- ❌ Cut 1 – ½" x 20" strip of fused fabric.
- ❌ Cut 4 – ½" x 2½" segments.
- ❌ Cut 8 – ½" x 1" segments.
- ❌ Cut 4 – 4" x 4" squares.
- ❌ Cut enough 2½" wide strips for a length of 42" (for the binding; join end-to-end).

From the tan felt:

- ❌ Cut 2 – ½" x 10" strips.
- ❌ Cut 20 – ½" x ½" squares.
- ❌ Cut 16 of the ½" x ½" squares in half once on the diagonal to make 32 triangles.

The top will have overhanging triangles that will be squared after the quilt is appliquéd.

Bear

❌ Trace the bear pattern (page 76) onto HeatnBond. Cut out ¼" beyond the line.

❌ Iron the bear shape to the wrong side of a scrap of blue fabric following the manufacturer's instructions. Cut on the line. Loosen a corner and remove the paper. Set aside.

Quilt Assembly

❌ Lay out the squares and triangles as shown. Sew into diagonal rows. Sew the rows together (Fig 1).

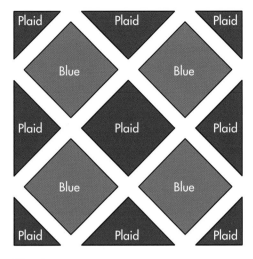

Fig. 1

❌ Fuse the bear to the center plaid square and appliqué in place with a buttonhole stitch.

❌ Press under ¼" on all 4 sides of the 4 – 3" x 3" red plaid squares. Center on the blue squares and appliqué in place with an invisible stitch (Fig. 2).

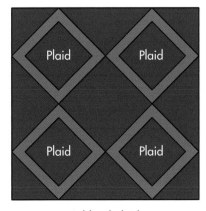

Add red plaid

Fig. 2

⊗ Position 1 – ½" x 2½" and 2 – ½" x 1" prepared blue segments on each of the red plaid squares, forming a cross. Fuse in place, then buttonhole stitch on all sides with blue thread (Fig 3).

⊗ Place a ½" x ½" tan felt square in the center of the cross and buttonhole stitch in place.

⊗ Position 16 felt triangles on the blue squares as shown and buttonhole stitch in place. Assemble blue denim look-alike fabric squares, red plaid squares, and red plaid triangles on point (Fig. 4).

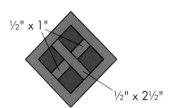

½" x 1"
½" x 2½"

Fig. 3

Add felt

Fig. 4

Finishing

⊗ Square up the quilt to measure 10½" x 10½". Layer with the batting and backing and thread or pin baste together.

⊗ Hand or machine quilt as shown. Trim the backing and batting even with the quilt (Fig. 5).

⊗ Sew the 4 red buttons onto the center tan squares and the black button onto the bear for its eye.

⊗ Fold the binding strip in half and attach to the completed quilt top using a ¼" seam. Turn to the back and hand finish.

⊗ Sew your label on the back in the bottom left corner.

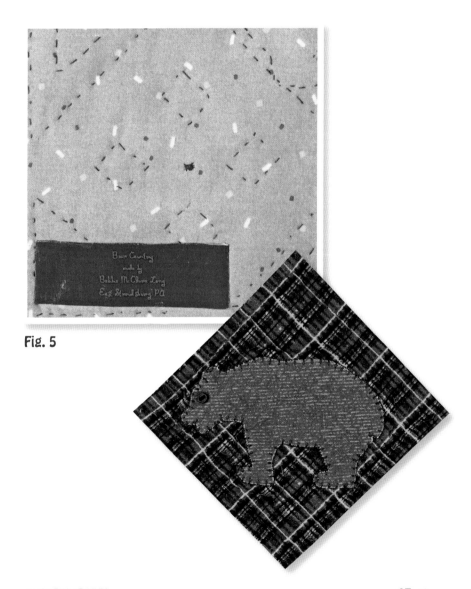

Fig. 5

Jake and
Geese of Many Colors

JAKE

Materials and Supplies

Clover yo-yo makers (small, large, extra large, and jumbo)

Basic yo-yo doll supplies (page 11)

1¼ yards bright print fabric

1¾ yards tan fabric

¼ yard brown fabric (for the body)

Scrap of solid green fabric (for the socks)

Scrap of solid brown fabric (for the shoes)

Black yarn (I used Lion Brand Homespun Yarn.)

¼ yard HeatnBond fusible interfacing

1 – ⁹/₁₆" half back covered button (for the nose)

2 – ½" white buttons (for the eyes)

2 small brown buttons (for the eyes)

2 – 2mm rhinestones (for the eyes)

4 brown rivets (for the shoes

Tortoiseshell glasses (optional)

Brown embroidery or craft thread

Making the Doll
Body

✳ Trace Jake's pattern (page 75). Make his head, hands, body, and face according to the general instructions (pages 12–13).

Yo-Yos

Fabric	# of squares	Size of squares	Yo-Yo Maker to Use	Placement
bright print	9	8½" x 8½"	Jumbo (blue)	torso
	14	5½" x 5½"	Extra large (yellow)	arms (6 each)
				neck (2)
	4	4½" x 4½"	Large (orange)	wrists (2 each)
tan	5	8½" x 8½"	Jumbo (blue)	torso
	44	5½" x 5½"	Extra large (yellow)	legs (22 each)
green	2	5½" x 5½"	Extra large (yellow)	socks
brown	2	5½" x 5½"	Extra large (yellow)	shoes

Cutting Instructions

For the jumbo yo-yos:

- ✪ Cut 3 – 8½" strips of bright print.
- ✪ Cut 9 – 8½" x 8½" squares.
- ✪ Cut 2 – 8½" strips of tan.
- ✪ Cut 5 – 8½" x 8½" squares.

For the extra-large yo-yos:

- ✪ Cut 2 – 5½" strips of bright print.
- ✪ Cut 14 – 5½" x 5½" squares.
- ✪ Cut 7 – 5½" strips of tan.
- ✪ Cut 44 – 5½" x 5½" squares.

For the large yo-yos:

- ✪ Cut 1 – 4½" strip of bright print.
- ✪ Cut 4 – 4½" x 4½" squares.

For the socks:

- ✪ Cut 2 green 5½" x 5½" squares.

For the shoes:

- ✪ Cut 2 brown 5½" x 5½" squares.

- ✪ Cut 14 – 2" x 2" squares and 62 – 1½" x 1½" squares of HeatnBond.

✪ Iron the larger squares of interfacing onto the center of the wrong side of the jumbo yo-yo fabric squares and the smaller squares onto the other yo-yo fabric squares, following the manufacturer's instructions. *The socks and shoes yo-yos don't need to be fused.*

✪ Cut a star-shaped opening in the center of the fused fabric squares (page 15), then peel off the paper.

✪ Insert the fabric squares into the appropriate size yo-yo makers and follow the manufacturer's instructions. Remember to leave an 8" tail of thread on 1 extra-large red plaid neck yo-yo; the 2 extra-large denim blue yo-yos for the ankles; the 2 large red plaid yo-yos for the wrists; and the shoes and socks yo-yos. They'll be cinched after they're added to the doll.

✪ Dress Jake with the yo-yos as described in Yo-Yos Dress the Doll (pages 15–17). Refer to the table (page 49) for placement of the yo-yos.

Finishing Touches

Hair

✪ Add the hair (page 17) and trim ½" long.

Shoes

✪ Insert 2 rivets in the front of each shoe following manufacturer's instructions.

✪ Lace brown embroidery or craft thread though the holes leaving about 5" tails on each side of the shoes.

✪ Put the shoes over each sock. Attach with a slipstitch and tie the laces. Double knot them and trim the tails to the length you want them.

Face

✪ Apply red chalk sparingly to Jake's cheeks with a chalk puff or Q-tip.

Glasses

✪ Shorten the arms of the glasses with a saw, then sand the rough edges.

GEESE OF MANY COLORS
9½" x 10", made by the author

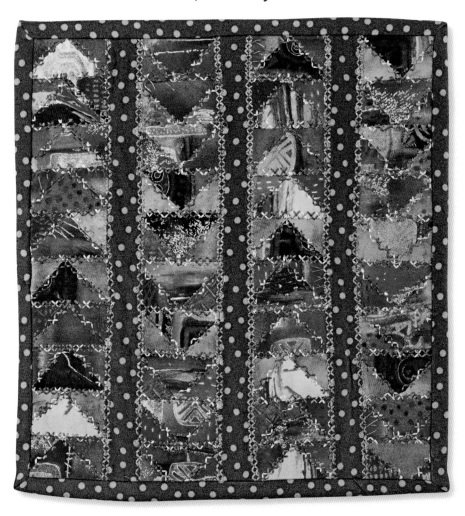

Jake really likes lots of bright colors and there are 40 bright geese in his quilt flying north and south. To make a quilt like Jake's, find the brightest and most varied fabric you can!

To cut down on bulk, use ⅛" seams.

Materials and Supplies

½ yard total of very colorful bright prints
    (I used one multicolored print fabric.)
11" x 11" backing
11" x 11" batting
Fat eighth of green polka dot for sashing and
    binding
Eleanor Burns Mini Geese One ruler
Quilt label (page 78)

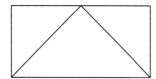

Fig. 1.

Fig. 2

Cutting Instructions

✳ Using the Mini Geese One ruler or the template (page 77), cut 40 geese and 80 wing triangles from the bright prints.

From the green polka dot:
✳ Cut 3 – 1" x 11" strips (for the sashing).
✳ Cut 2 – 2½" x 22" strips and join end-to-end (for the binding).

Making the Quilt

✳ Join the triangles as shown to make 40 Flying Geese units (Fig. 1).

✳ Lay out the Flying Geese units in 4 vertical rows of 10 each. Join with ⅛" seams.

✳ Join the rows with the 3 sashing strips, alternating the direction of the geese as shown (Fig. 2).

Finishing

✳ Pin the quilt top to the batting.

✳ Stitch around each of the geese and on both sides of the sashing strips with variegated bright thread. I used the crisscross decorative stitch.

✳ Iron the quilt top to the backing. Trim the batting and backing even with the quilt top.

✳ Fold the binding strip in half and attach to the completed quilt top using a ¼" seam. Turn to the back and hand finish.

✳ Sew your label on the back in the bottom left corner.

Charlie and Stellar Steelers

CHARLIE

Materials and Supplies

Clover yo-yo makers (small, large, and extra large)

Basic yo-yo doll supplies (page 11)

⅓ yard Pittsburgh Steelers* NFL fabric; includes yardage for Charlie's quilt (see Resources, page 78)

⅝ yard blue*

½ yard black*

⅓ yard yellow*

⅓ yard white*

¼ yard ivory (for the body)

Brown yarn (I used Lion Brand Homespun Yarn in Barley.)

⅛ yard HeatnBond fusible interfacing

1 – ⁷⁄₁₆" half back covered button (for the nose)

White embroidery or craft thread

1 – ⁹⁄₁₆" half back covered button (for the baseball cap)

2 – small white buttons (for the eyes)

2 – small blue buttons (for the eyes)

2 – 2mm rhinestones (for the eyes)

8 white rivets (for the shoes)

*Or choose your favorite team and alter the fabric colors accordingly.

Yo-Yos

Fabric	# of squares	Size of squares	Yo-Yo Maker to Use	Placement
black	4	5½" x 5½"	Extra large (yellow)	torso
	10	4½" x 4½"	Large (orange)	arms (2 each)
				shoes (2 each)
				neck (1)
				hat (1)
	2	3" x 3"	Small (blue)	wrists (1 each)
white	2	5½" x 5½"	Extra large (yellow)	torso
	4	4½" x 4½"	Large (orange)	arms (2 each)
	4	3" x 3"	Small (green)	shoes soles (2 each)
yellow	2	5½" x 5½"	Extra large (yellow)	torso
	4	4½" x 4½"	Large (orange)	arms (1 each)
				socks (2)
blue	4	5½" x 5½"	Extra large (yellow)	torso
	24	4½" x 4½"	Large (orange)	legs (12 each)

Making the Doll

⊗ Trace Charlie's pattern (page 75). Make his head, hands, body, and face according to the general instructions (pages 12–13).

Cutting Instructions

For the extra-large yo-yos:

⊗ Cut 1 – 5½" black strip.
⊗ Cut 4 – 5½" x 5½" squares.
⊗ Cut 1 – 5½" white strip.
⊗ Cut 2 – 5½" x 5½" squares.
⊗ Cut 1 – 5½" yellow strip.
⊗ Cut 2 – 5½" x 5½" squares.
⊗ Cut 1 – 5½" blue strip.
⊗ Cut 4 – 5½" x 5½" squares.

For the large yo-yos:

⊗ Cut 2 – 4½" black strips.
⊗ Cut 10 – 4½" x 4½" squares.
⊗ Cut 1 – 4½" white strip.
⊗ Cut 4– 4½" x 4½" squares.
⊗ Cut 1 – 4½" yellow strip.
⊗ Cut 4 – 4½" x 4½" squares.
⊗ Cut 3 – 4½" blue strips.
⊗ Cut 24 – 4½" x 4½" squares.

For the small yo-yos:

⊗ Cut 2 – 3" x 3" black squares.
⊗ Cut 2 – 3" x 3" white squares.
⊗ Cut 49 1½" x 1½" squares of HeatnBond.

⊗ Iron the squares of interfacing onto the center of the wrong side of the yo-yo fabric squares, following the manufacturer's instructions. *The socks, shoes, shoe soles, and hat yo-yos don't need to be fused.*

⊗ Cut a star-shaped opening in the center of the fused fabric squares (page 15), then peel off the paper.

⊗ Insert the fabric squares into the appropriate size yo-yo makers and follow the manufacturer's instructions. Leave an 8" tail of thread on 1 large black neck yo-yo; the 2 small black wrist yo-yos; the large blue ankle yo-yos; and the shoes, soles, and socks yo-yos. They'll be cinched after they're added to the doll. All the other yo-yos can be cinched shut leaving about a half-inch opening.

⊗ Dress Charlie, keeping in mind that his yo-yos are one size smaller than indicated in Yo-Yos Dress the Doll (pages 15–17). Refer to the yo-yos table (page 54) and Charlie's photo for placement of the yo-yos.

Finishing Touches

Hair

✳ Add the hair (page 17). Do not cut slits in the area of Charlie's head where his hat will sit. Leave a small "bald" spot there. Trim his hair ½" long.

Baseball Cap

✳ For the brim, cut 2 half circles (page 75) of black fabric. Sew right sides together and turn. Slipstitch the brim onto Charlie's head.

✳ Cover the ⁷⁄₁₆" button with the Steelers' logo. Attach the covered button to a large black yo-yo for the crown. Make a small pleat where the button is attached and sew to the brim. Slipstitch the yo-yo to Charlie's head.

Shoes

✳ Insert 4 rivets in the front of each shoe following the manufacturer's instructions.

✳ Lace white embroidery or craft thread though the holes leaving about 5" tails on each side of the shoes.

✳ Put the shoes over each sock. Attach with a slipstitch and tie the laces. Double knot them and trim the tails to the length you want them.

✳ Cinch the 2 small white yo-yos to a size that will cover the bottom of Charlie's shoes. Slipstitch in place.

Face

✳ Apply pink chalk to his cheeks with a chalk puff or a Q-tip.

STELLAR STEELERS

9½" x 9½", made by the author

Charlie is a big Pittsburgh Steelers fan so his quilt is made in the Steelers' colors of yellow and black. Other fabric and colors of your favorite team can be substituted. If you cannot find the NFL fabric of your choice, see Resources (page 78) for an Internet source.

Materials and Supplies

⅓ yard Pittsburgh Steelers NFL fabric (for the logos and backing)

Fat quarter black (for blocks and binding)

Fat quarter yellow (for the blocks)

Scraps of white (to line the team logos)

¼ yard HeatnBond fusible interfacing

10½" x 10½" batting

Multicolored 2mm rhinestones

Quilt label (page 78)

Making the Quilt
Cutting Instructions
From the black:
- ✪ Cut 1 strip 1½" wide (for the four-patch units).
- ✪ Cut 1 strip 2½" wide into 4 – 2½" x 2½" squares (for the blocks).
- ✪ Cut 2 strips 1" wide (for the border strip-sets).
- ✪ Cut 1 strip 2" wide into 4 – 2" x 2" squares (for the cornerstones).
- ✪ Cut 2 strips 2½" wide (for the binding; join end-to-end).

From the yellow:
- ✪ Cut 4 strips 1" wide (for the border strip-sets).
- ✪ Cut 1 strip 1½" wide (for the four-patch units).

From the team fabric:
- ✪ Cut a 10½" x 10½" square (for the backing).

Preparing the Team Logos
- ✪ Fuse HeatnBond to the back of the NFL logos.

- ✪ Cut 9 team logos, leaving an extra bit of fabric around each one:
    4 – 1½" logos
    4 – 1" logos
    1 – ¾" logo

- ✪ Loosen one edge of the paper and remove. Fuse the logos to white fabric. Fuse interfacing to the back of the white fabric and cut out the logos precisely. Remove the paper.

Piecing the Top
- ✪ Make one strip-set with the yellow and black 1½" strips. Cut 10 – 1½" segments. Join 2 segments into a four-patch unit. Make 5 (Fig. 1).

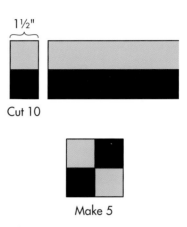

1½"

Cut 10

Make 5

Fig. 1

- ✪ Lay out the four-patch units and 2½" black squares in a nine-patch arrangement as shown. Join the blocks into rows and join the rows (Fig. 2).

- ✪ Fuse the 1½" logos in the center of the black squares and the ¾" logo in the center of the middle four-patch.

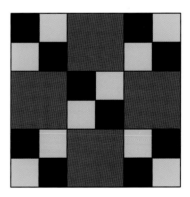

Fig. 2

✪ Make 2 strip-sets with the yellow and black 1" strips. Cut 4 – 6" segments (Fig. 3).

✪ Add 2 segments to opposite sides of the quilt top.

✪ Add the 2" black squares to the ends of the remaining strip-set segments and add to the other 2 sides of the quilt top. Fuse the 1" logos to the cornerstones.

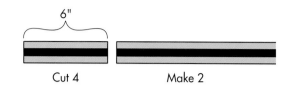

Fig. 3

Finishing

✪ Pin the quilt top to the batting.

✪ Buttonhole stitch around each of the logos.

✪ Heat-fix the red, yellow, and blue rhinestones to the center of each diamond shape in each logo.

✪ Add diagonal quilting through the centers of the blocks, stopping at each logo and continuing on its opposite side.

✪ Layer the top and batting with the backing.

✪ Trim the backing and batting even with the quilt top and add the binding.

✪ Fold under one long side of the binding ¼" and press. Sew the unfolded edge of the binding to the quilt with a ¼" seam. Fold the binding to the back and hand finish. Stitch in the ditch in the borders, which will secure the binding on the back.

✪ Sew your label on the back in the bottom left corner.

Willa Jane and
The Other Potter

WILLA JANE

Materials and Supplies

Clover yo-yo makers (extra small, small, and large)

Basic yo-yo doll supplies (page 11)

⅛ yard HeatnBond fusible interfacing

½ yard pink novelty print: includes yardage for Willa Jane's quilt (I used Quilting Treasures™ by Cranston, Beatrix Potter Garden Tales collection 25553-P.)

Scrap of light pink polka-dot fabric (for the bonnet)

Yellow yarn (I used Lion Brand Homespun Yarn in Sunshine State.)

2 – small white buttons (for the eyes)

2 – small blue buttons (for the eyes)

2 – 2mm rhinestones (for the eyes)

⅔ yard half-inch pink satin ribbon

Making the Doll
Body

Trace Willa Jane's pattern (page 74). Make her head, hands, body, and face according to the general instructions (pages 12–13).

Cutting Instructions

For the large yo-yos:
- Cut 1 – 4½" strip of pink print.
- Cut 6 – 4½" x 4½" squares.

For the small yo-yos:
- Cut 2 – 3" strips of pink print.
- Cut 25 – 3" x 3" squares.
- Cut 1 – 3" x 3" pink polka-dot square.

For the extra-small yo-yos:
- Cut 2 – 2½" x 2½" squares of pink print.
- Cut 31 – 1½" x ½" squares of HeatnBond.

Yo-Yos

Fabric	# of squares	Size of squares	Yo-Yo Maker to Use	Placement
pink novelty print	6	4½" x 4½"	Large (orange)	torso
	25	3" x 3"	Small (green)	arms (5 each)
				legs (6 each)
				neck (1)
				booties (2)
	2	2½" x 2½"	Extra Small (blue)	ankles
pink polka dot	1	3" x 3"	Small (green)	bonnet

✪ Iron the squares of interfacing onto the center of the wrong side of the yo-yo fabric squares, following the manufacturer's instructions. *The booties and bonnet yo-yos don't need to be fused.*

✪ Cut a star-shaped opening in the center of the fused fabric squares (page 15), then peel off the paper.

✪ Insert the fabric squares into the appropriate size yo-yo makers and follow the manufacturer's instructions. Leave an 8" tail of thread on 1 small neck yo-yo; 2 extra-small ankle yo-yos; 4 small yo-yos for the arms and booties; and the small bonnet yo-yo. They'll be cinched after they're added to the doll. All the other yo-yos can be cinched shut leaving about a half-inch opening.

✪ Dress Willa Jane, keeping in mind that her yo-yos are two sizes smaller than indicated in Yo-Yos Dress the Doll (pages 15–17). Refer to the yo-yos table (page 61) for placement of the yo-yos.

Note: The booties are added like socks (page 16). Tie a pink ribbon around the ankles after stitching the booties in place.

Finishing Touches
Bonnet

✪ Cut a 3¼" x 3½" pink polka-dot rectangle.

✪ Cut a 1½" x 3" rectangle of HeatnBond and fuse to the back of the polka-dot rectangle as shown (Fig. 1).

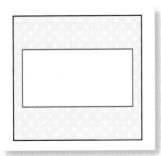

Fig. 1

✪ Remove the paper. Fold the rectangle in half. Tuck in the ends and fuse to form the bonnet brim.

✪ Sew a 5" piece of ribbon at both ends of the rectangle.

✪ Place the brim on Willa Jane's head and tie the ribbon into a bow under her chin. Slipstitch the brim to her head and trim the ends of the ribbon.

✪ Slipstitch the small pink polka-dot yo-yo to the brim and to the back of Willa Jane's head. Make a small bow of pink ribbon and stitch over the yo-yo opening (Fig. 2).

Fig. 2

Hair

✪ Add bangs and hair above where her ears would be (page 17). Trim to ½" long.

Face

✪ Make one tiny traditional yo-yo and stuff it lightly with fiberfill for the nose. Sew in place.

✪ Apply pink chalk to her cheeks with a chalk puff or a Q-tip.

THE OTHER POTTER

8½" x 8½", made by the author

The blocks and cornerstones are fussy cut to position the motifs in the center. I used Beatrix Potter Garden Tales Collection 25551-B and 25553-P from Quilting Treasures, but you can use any novelty fabric you like.

My Aunt Wilma made many, many dolls, doll dresses, and quilts that have been treasured for generations. This one's for you, Aunt Wilma!

Materials and Supplies

⅓ yard novelty fabric
⅛ yard coordinating fabric for sashing and binding
9½" x 9½" flannel for backing
9½" x 9½" batting
⅛ yard HeatnBond fusible interfacing
Quilt label (page 78)

Cutting Instructions

From the novelty fabric*:

- ✱ Fussy cut 4 – 3" x 3" squares (for the blocks).
- ✱ Fussy cut 9 – 1½" x 1½" squares (for the cornerstones).
- ✱ Cut 1 – 2½" x 40" strip (for the binding).

*I cut oval motifs from the Beatrix Potter fabric, fused them to 3" x 3" squares of coordinating background fabric, and buttonhole stitched around **both** the *outside* and the *inside* of the oval frame edges, making it look like I sewed the picture and frame individually.

✱ If you want separate motifs for the blocks, fuse HeatnBond to the back of the fabric before cutting out the motifs.

From the coordinating fabric:

- ✱ Cut 12 – 1½" x 3" strips (for the sashing).

Making the Quilt

✱ Arrange the squares, cornerstones, and sashing strips in rows as shown. If you cut separate motifs, fuse them to the squares first (Fig. 1).

✱ Sew the components into rows, then join the rows.

✱ Pin the quilt top in the center of the batting.

✱ Stitch in the ditch with coordinating variegated pastel thread. I used a crisscross decorative stitch.

✱ Using the same decorative stitch and matching thread, stitch through the middle of the sashing strips.

Finishing

✱ Iron the quilt top and batting to a 9½" x 9½" square of flannel backing.

✱ Trim the batting and backing even with the quilt top.

✱ Fold the binding strip in half and attach to the completed quilt top using a ¼" seam.

✱ Turn to the back and hand finish.

✱ Add a label in the lower left corner.

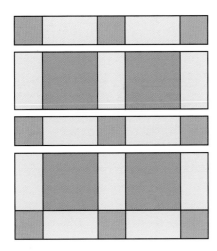

Fig. 1

JUNO THE DOG

Juno the Dog

Materials and Supplies

Clover yo-yo makers (extra small, small, large, extra large, and jumbo)

Basic yo-yo doll supplies (page 11)

¾ yard 60" wide brown fake fur

¾ yard 60" wide white fake fur

⅓ yard white cotton (for the body)

Scrap of black fleece (for the nose)

¼ yard HeatnBond fusible interfacing

2 – ⅝" brown buttons (for the eyes)

2 – 2mm rhinestones (for the eyes)

14 – 4mm assorted rhinestones (for the collar)

Small dog collar

White bone charm with rhinestones (for the collar)

1 – 1½" circle template

5 feet of 14-gauge electrical wire

Wire cutters

Electrical tape

Pliers

Juno is our granddog. Yo-Yo Juno is a lot smaller and is not as vocal or as lively as her namesake, but she does articulate! She is a chubby little puppy that can sit up and beg for you to pet her soft fur. She is made with a strong inner core of electrical wire. The wire gives her the added sturdiness some puppies need. She can, however, be made without the armature, giving her a softer look. She is hard to resist.

Preparing the Parts
Body

⊗ Copy and cut out the dog pattern (page 76), taping the halves together as indicated.

⊗ Cut out 2 bodies, placing the long edge along a fold as indicated.

⊗ Sew the 2 bodies right sides together. Leave an opening under the torso from the front to the back legs, backstitching at the beginning and the end.

⊗ Turn right-side out using an unsharpened pencil or commercial fabric turner.

Armature

⊗ For the head and body, cut a 14" piece of wire. Form a small loop 6" from one end (for the front legs). Form a loop 1½" in diameter at the other end for the head.

⊗ For the front legs, cut a 14" piece of wire. Insert 7" through the small loop in the body. Tighten the loop with pliers and wrap the joint securely with electrical tape.

⊗ For the back legs, cut a 14" piece of wire. Form a small loop on the tail end of the body wire. Insert 7" of wire through the loop. Tighten the loop with pliers and wrap the joint securely with electrical tape.

⊗ Bend the wire at the end of each leg inward the body, forming a small loop (Fig. 1).

⊗ Put the armature inside Juno's body and bend the legs into shape.

Fig. 1

⊗ Stuff the body around the wire with fiberfill using the handle of a wooden spoon. Sew the opening closed by hand.

Ears

⊗ Trace and cut out the ear pattern (page 76).

⊗ Trace 2 ears onto both the brown and white fake fur (total 4) and cut out.

⊗ Sew the pairs right sides together, leaving the bottom open.

⊗ Turn right-sides out and slipstitch the bottom closed on each ear. Set aside.

Eye Patch

⊗ Trace and cut out the eye patch pattern (page 76).

⊗ Trace the eye patch onto a scrap of brown fake fur and cut out.

⊗ Fold under ¼" along the straight sides and press. Set aside.

Tail

⊗ Trace and cut out the tail patterns (page 76).

⊗ Trace 2 lower tail pieces on brown fake fur and trace 2 tail tip pieces on white fake fur. Cut out.

⊗ Join the 2 tail tip pieces with a ¼" seam along the outside arc. Repeat with the 2 lower tail pieces. Finger press the seams open.

⊗ Sew the 2 tail sections right sides together, aligning the center seams. The white tip of the tail will look like it doesn't fit. Sew from one edge to the seam. With the needle down, adjust the remaining half and sew to the end.

⊗ With right sides together, partially sew the last seam from the tip of the tail. Turn right-side out and finish the seam by hand.

⊗ Stuff with fiberfill and set aside.

Yo-Yos

Fabric	# of squares	Size of squares	Yo-Yo Maker to Use	Placement
white fake fur	1	12½" x 12½"	Oversized (traditional method)	head
	3	8½" x 8½"	Jumbo (blue)	body
	13	5½" x 5½"	Extra large (yellow)	muzzle (1)
				neck (2)
				front legs (3 each)
				feet (4)
	10	4½" x 4½"	Large (orange)	base of front legs
				(2 each)
				base of hind legs (3 each)
	1	3" x 3"	Small (green)	muzzle
brown fake fur	9	8½" x 8½"	Jumbo (blue)	body (7)
				top of hind legs (1 each)
	6	5½" x 5½"	Extra large (yellow)	front legs (1 each)
				hind legs (2 each)
	8	4½" x 4½"	Large (orange)	front legs (2 each)
				hind legs (2 each)
black fleece	1	2½" x 2½"	Extra small (blue)	nose

Cutting Instructions

For the oversized yo-yo:
- Cut 1 – 12½" x 12½" square of white fake fur.
- Trace the outline of a 12" circle onto the fabric and cut out the circle.

For the jumbo yo-yos:
- Cut 1 – 8½" strip of white fake fur.
- Cut 3 – 8½" x 8½" squares.
- Cut 2 – 8½" strips of brown fake fur.
- Cut 9 – 8½" x 8½" squares.

For the extra-large yo-yos:
- Cut 2 – 5½" strips of white fake fur.
- Cut 13 – 5½" x 5½" squares.
- Cut 1 – 5½" strip of brown fake fur.
- Cut 6 – 5½" x 5½" squares.

For the large yo-yos:
- Cut 2 – 4½" strips of white fake fur.
- Cut 10 – 4½" x 4½" squares.
- Cut 1 – 4½" strip of brown fake fur.
- Cut 8 – 4½" x 4½" squares.

For the small yo-yo:
- Cut 1 – 3" x 3" square of white fake fur.

For the extra small yo-yo:
- Cut 1 – 2½" x 2½" square of black fleece.

- Cut 12 – 2" x 2" squares of HeatnBond.
- Cut 32 – 1½" x 1½" squares of Heatn-Bond.

❁ Iron the larger squares of interfacing onto the center of the wrong side of the jumbo yo-yo fabric circles and the smaller squares onto the yo-yo fabric squares, following the manufacturer's instructions.

The 4 yo-yos for the feet and 4 yo-yos used for the head, muzzle (2), and nose do not need to be fused.

❁ Cut a star-shaped opening in the center of the fused fabric squares (page 15), then peel off the paper. Cut larger stars in the bigger body yo-yo squares and smaller stars in leg yo-yo squares.

❁ Insert the fabric squares into the appropriate size yo-yo makers and follow the manufacturer's instructions. Leave a 10" tail of thread on the nose, 2 muzzle, and 4 feet yo-yos to stuff with fiberfill and attach later. All the other yo-yos can be cinched shut. Leave about ½" opening on the leg yo-yos, and a slightly larger opening on the body yo-yos.

Adding the Yo-Yos
Head

❁ Cut an 11½" circle out of the 12" square of white fake fur.

❁ Sew the eye patch to the circle, aligning the raw edges. Slipstitch the folded edges of the eye patch to the circle by hand.

❁ Make an oversized yo-yo out of the circle using the traditional method, leaving a long tail of thread. Loosely cinch the opening. Tightly wrap the side opposite the opening with a rubber band. (The rubber band will be covered by the muzzle.)

❁ Color a pupil around the buttonholes on the brown button eyes with a black fine-line permanent pen. Sew the eyes onto the face as shown (Fig. 2).

❁ Stuff the small mouth yo-yo with fiberfill and slipstitch in place as shown (Fig. 2).

❁ Stuff the extra-large muzzle yo-yo with fiberfill and slipstitch in place just below the eyes and on top of the small mouth yo-yo, covering the rubber band and leaving the bottom of the mouth showing.

❁ Stuff the nose yo-yo and slipstitch in place.

❁ Position the ears on the side of the head ¼" from the eyes and slipstitch in place. Set aside.

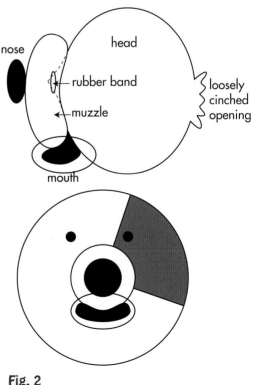

Fig. 2

Body

❂ When adding yo-yos to Juno's body, the cinched opening should be toward the head and face-up on the legs. Refer to the placement diagram for the color sequence of the yo-yos.

❂ Add 9 jumbo yo-yos to the body. Place over one hind leg, then bend the other leg to slide the yo-yo up to the torso. Bend the leg back into position before adding the tail and leg yo-yos.

❂ Sew the tail to the torso.

❂ Add the leg yo-yos. Slipstitch the top leg yo-yos to the last brown torso yo-yo, leaving just a bit of the last white torso yo-yo showing. Slipstitch the top leg yo-yos together beneath the tail.

❂ Stuff the 4 feet yo-yos with fiberfill. Add to the bottom of each leg, cinch closed, and hand sew securely in place.

❂ Add the 3 neck yo-yos (Fig. 3).

❂ Sew the head firmly onto the neck, inserting a doll needle and thread through the neck front to the back and side to side, pulling the head as close to the body as you can. Slipstitch around the bottom of the head to secure it to the neck.

Finishing touches

❂ Add 1 – 2mm rhinestone to each eye to give the doll twinkling eyes.

❂ Add 4mm assorted bright color rhinestones evenly around the collar. Adjust the dog collar to fit around Juno's neck and attach a white bone charm with rhinestones to the collar.

Tip: If you don't use an armature, sew the top of the front and hind leg yo-yos together, using a doll needle, to give added support to the legs.

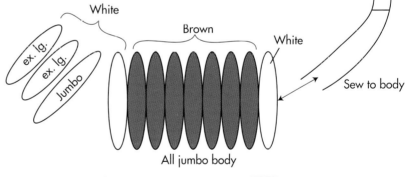

All jumbo body

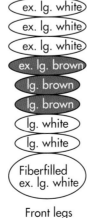

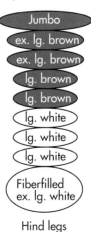

Fig.3   Front legs   Hind legs

MISSY THE CAT

Missy the Cat

Materials and Supplies

Clover yo-yo makers (extra small, small, large, extra large, and jumbo)

Basic yo-yo doll supplies (page 11)

1½ yards of 60" wide fun fur

⅓ yard pink cotton (for the body)

⅓ yard purple cotton (for yo-yo lining and tail armature)

Scrap of pink fleece (for the nose)

Scrap of purple fleece (for the ears)

2 – ⅝" green buttons (for the eyes)

2 – 2mm rhinestones (for the eyes)

17 – 4mm rhinestones (clear, pink, and purple)

1 – 5mm clear rhinestone

3½" animal whiskers

Hot pink small cat collar with bell

Silver charm with pink rhinestone

12" of 9-gauge aluminum wire

Wire cutters

Yo-Yo Missy may seem a little otherworldly with her fur made of unusual colors. That is because she is. Mistletoe came to us on Christmas Eve twenty years ago. She went on to another life last year. This Yo-Yo Missy was made to celebrate her life. She was never a typical cat in this life so why should she be in the next one?

Preparing the Parts
Body

✖ Copy and cut out the cat pattern (page 77).

✖ Cut out 2 bodies from the pink cotton, placing the long edge along a fold as indicated.

✖ Sew the 2 bodies right sides together. Leave an opening under the torso from the front to the back legs, backstitching at the beginning and the end of the opening.

✖ Turn right-side out using an unsharpened pencil or commercial fabric turner.

✖ Stuff the body firmly with fiberfill using the handle of a wooden spoon. Sew the opening closed by hand. Set aside.

Ears

✖ Trace and cut out the ear pattern (page 77).

✖ Trace 2 ears onto both the fun fur and purple fleece (total 4) and cut out.

✖ Sew an ear of fur and fleece right sides together, leaving the bottom open. Repeat.

✖ Turn right-sides out and slipstitch the bottom closed on each ear. Set aside.

Tail Armature

✖ Cut a 13" x 2½" strip of purple fabric.

✖ Fold in half with right sides together. Sew across one end and along the side, backstitching where you started and stopped, to form a tube. Turn right-side out.

✖ Insert a 12" piece of aluminum wire into the tube. Tuck in the unfinished end and slipstitch closed.

Cutting Instructions
For the oversized yo-yo:

✖ Cut 1 – 12½" x 12½" square of fun fur.

✖ Trace the outline of a 12" circle onto the fabric and cut out the circle.

✖ Cut 1 – 12½" square of purple to line the head yo-yo.

✖ Trace the outline of a 12" circle onto the fabric and cut out the circle.

For the jumbo yo-yos:

✖ Cut 2 – 8½" strips of fun fur.

✖ Cut 11 – 8½" x 8½" squares.

✖ Cut 1 – 8½" x 8½" square of purple to line the face yo-yo.

Yo-Yos

Fabric	# of squares	Size of squares	Yo-Yo Maker to Use	Placement
fun fur	1	12½" x 12½"	Oversized (traditional method)	head
	10	8½" x 8½"	Jumbo (blue)	body
	37	5½" x 5½"	Extra large (yellow)	neck (1)
				legs (8 each)
				feet (4)
	13	4½" x 4½"	Large (orange)	mouth (1)
				ankles (4)
				tail (6)
				neck (2)
	14	3" x 3"	Small (green)	cheeks (2)
				tail (12)
pink fleece	1	2½" x 2½"	Extra small (blue)	nose (1)

For the extra large yo-yos:

- ❌ Cut 4 – 5½" strips of fun fur.
- ❌ Cut 38 – 5½" x 5½" squares.
- ❌ Cut 1 – 8½" strip of purple cotton.
- ❌ Cut 4 – 8½" x 8½" squares to line the 4 feet yo-yos.

For the large yo-yos:

- ❌ Cut 1 – 4½" strip of fun fur.
- ❌ Cut 10 – 4½" x 4½" squares.
- ❌ Cut 2 – 4½" x 4½" squares of purple cotton to line the mouth and end of tail yo-yos.

For the small yo-yo:

- ❌ Cut 1 – 3" strip of fun fur.
- ❌ Cut 14 – 3" x 3" squares.
- ❌ Cut 2 – 3" x 3" squares of purple cotton to line the cheeks yo-yos.

For the extra small yo-yo:

- ❌ Cut 1 – 2½" x 2½" square of pink fleece.

❌ Make the following yo-yos by layering the fun fur and purple lining squares together. Stuff with fiberfill, leaving a 10" thread tail for tightening up later, and set aside.

  1 jumbo yo-yo for the face

  4 extra-large yo-yos for the feet

  2 large yo-yos for the mouth and tip of the tail

  2 small yo-yos for the cheeks

- ❌ Make and lightly stuff the extra-small nose yo-yo and cinch closed.
- ❌ Cut 10 – 2" x 2" squares of HeatnBond.
- ❌ Cut 54 – 1½" x 1½" squares of Heatn-Bond.

❌ Iron the larger squares of interfacing onto the center of the wrong side of the jumbo yo-yo squares and the smaller squares onto the other yo-yo squares, following the manufacturer's instructions.

❌ Cut a star-shaped opening in the center of the fused fabric squares (page 15), then peel off the paper. Cut larger stars in the bigger body yo-yo squares and smaller stars in the leg yo-yo squares.

❌ Insert the fabric squares into the appropriate size yo-yo makers and follow the manufacturer's instructions. Leave about a ½" opening on all the yo-yos.

Adding the Yo-Yos

When adding yo-yos to Missy's body, the cinched opening should be toward the head and face-up on the legs. On the tail, the cinched opening should face the end of the tail.

❌ Add the 9 jumbo yo-yos to the body, sliding them over the hind legs and up to the neck.

❌ Sew the top of the front and hind legs together using a doll needle to give added support to the legs.

❌ Add the leg yo-yos as shown (Fig. 1, page 73).

❌ Sew a large stuffed yo-yo to the end of the tail. Add 5 large and 12 small yo-yos as shown. Bend the tail at the spot between the large and small yo-yos. Slide the small yo-yos 5" from the end and bend the tail in the opposite direction.

❌ Insert 5" of the tail armature through the yo-yos on the top of the cat's back. Using a long doll needle, sew loops around the armature and through the cat's body (Fig. 1, page 73).

❌ Add the neck yo-yos as shown.

❌ Color slit-shaped pupils on the eye buttons and sew half way down the face. Slipstitch the large lightly stuffed mouth yo-yo in the center of the face directly under the eyes.

✪ Stuff the traditional oversized yo-yo for the head. Loosely cinch closed.

✪ Make a small hole slightly off-center through the 2 small stuffed cheek yo-yos. Insert the whiskers and tack them in place. Slipstitch the yo-yos side-by-side on the top part of Missy's mouth, making sure the bottom of the mouth shows.

✪ Sew the head on the body.

✪ Slipstitch the nose yo-yo between and slightly higher than the cheeks.

✪ Slipstitch the ears on top of the head.

✪ Sew the head onto the neck, pulling it as close to the body as you can. Slipstitch around the bottom of the head, inserting a doll needle and thread through the neck, front to back and side to side.

RIGHT: Snowball was made just like Missy. Her fur is thicker, so it took fewer yo-yos.

Finishing Touches

✪ Add one 2mm rhinestone to each eye.

✪ Adjust the cat collar to fit around her neck. Add 4mm clear, pink, and purple rhinestones evenly around the collar.

✪ Add one 6mm clear rhinestone in the center of the clasp.

✪ Attach the silver heart charm to the collar buckle.

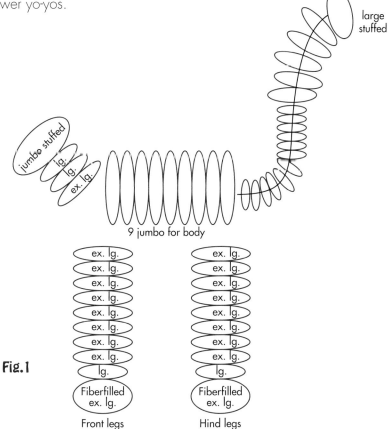

large stuffed

jumbo stuffed
lg.
lg.
ex. lg.

9 jumbo for body

Front legs	Hind legs
ex. lg.	ex. lg.
ex. lg.	ex. lg.
ex. lg.	ex. lg.
ex. lg.	ex. lg.
ex. lg.	ex. lg.
ex. lg.	ex. lg.
ex. lg.	ex. lg.
ex. lg.	ex. lg.
lg.	lg.
Fiberfilled ex. lg.	Fiberfilled ex. lg.

Fig.1

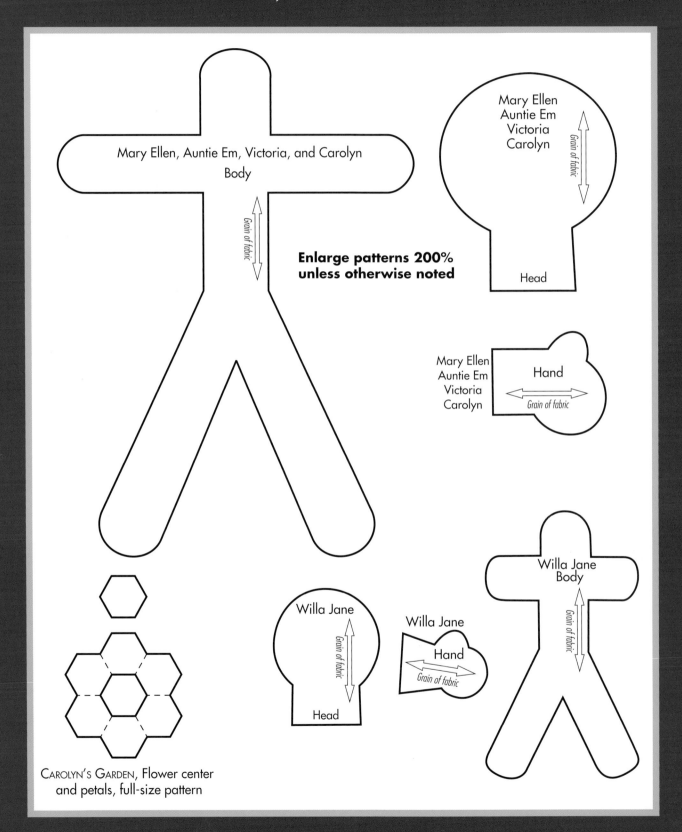

Mary Ellen, Auntie Em, Victoria, and Carolyn
Body

Grain of fabric

Mary Ellen
Auntie Em
Victoria
Carolyn

Grain of fabric

Head

Enlarge patterns 200% unless otherwise noted

Mary Ellen
Auntie Em
Victoria
Carolyn

Hand

Grain of fabric

Willa Jane
Body

Grain of fabric

Willa Jane

Grain of fabric

Head

Willa Jane

Hand

Grain of fabric

CAROLYN'S GARDEN, Flower center
and petals, full-size pattern

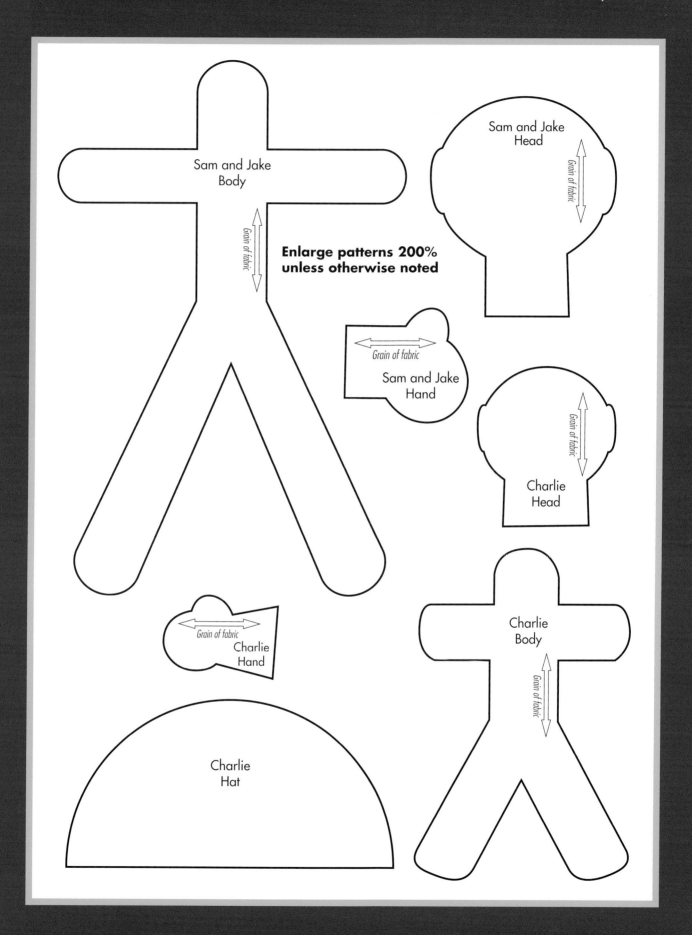

Sam and Jake
Body

Sam and Jake
Head

Grain of fabric

**Enlarge patterns 200%
unless otherwise noted**

Grain of fabric

Grain of fabric

Sam and Jake
Hand

Grain of fabric

Charlie
Head

Grain of fabric

Charlie
Body

Charlie
Hand

Grain of fabric

Charlie
Hat

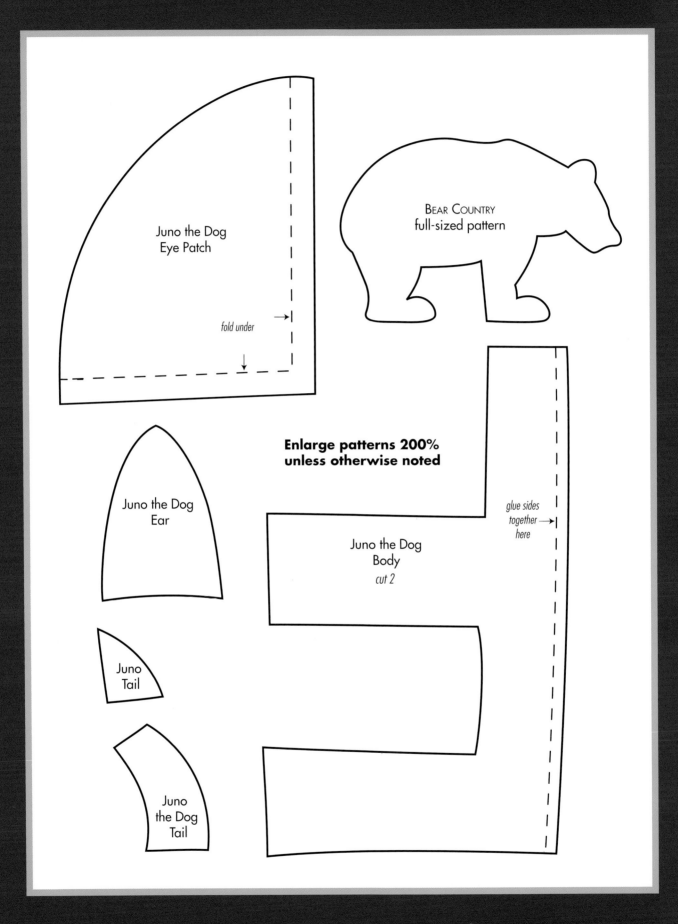

Juno the Dog
Eye Patch

fold under →

↓

Bear Country
full-sized pattern

Enlarge patterns 200%
unless otherwise noted

Juno the Dog
Ear

Juno the Dog
Body
cut 2

*glue sides
together* →
here

Juno
Tail

Juno
the Dog
Tail

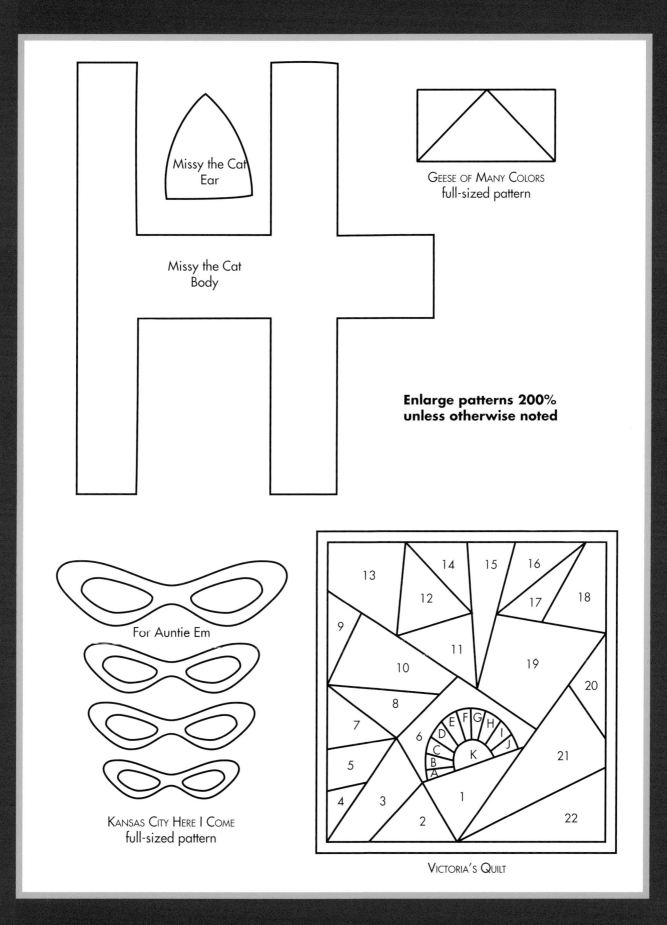

Missy the Cat
Ear

Missy the Cat
Body

GEESE OF MANY COLORS
full-sized pattern

**Enlarge patterns 200%
unless otherwise noted**

For Auntie Em

KANSAS CITY HERE I COME
full-sized pattern

VICTORIA'S QUILT

Making Labels

Make all the labels for the quilts at the same time using a graphic computer program of your choice that allows you to add your own words and shapes.

- Make 8 white 1½" x 3½" rectangles.

- Make 8 – 1" x 3" rectangles and center them in larger white rectangles.

- Color each of these center rectangles whatever color matches your quilt the best.

- Add a text box in the center of one of the colored rectangles and stretch its edges to fit inside that box.

- Choose the font style and size for the lettering.

- Include the name of the quilt, your name and address, and the date. Center the text.

- After you have made the first label, highlight it, duplicate it, move it to the next box and only change the quilt name and whatever else you want different from the first label.

- Test on a sheet of plain white printer paper. When you are happy with the results, insert paper-backed fabric into your ink-jet printer, following the manufacturer's instructions.

- Cut each label out along the outside line.

- Fold under the edges along the inside lines, lightly iron the labels, and they are ready to sew on the little quilts.

Everyone will want to know where you got the cute little labels!

Resources

Artbeads.com®
11901 137th Ave. Ct. KPN
Gig Harbor, Washington 98329
Phone: 866.715.BEAD (2323)
Web site:
http://www.artbeads.com
for rhinestones, beads, and Stretch Magic Bead and Jewelry Cord

J&O Fabrics Center, Inc.
9401 Rt 130 South
Pennsauken, NJ 08110
Phone: 856-663-2121
Web site:
http://www.jandofabrics.com
for NFL team fabrics

Quilting Treasures™
2 Worcester Road
Webster, MA 01570
Phone: 1-800-876-2756
Web site:
http://www.
quiltingtreasures.com
for Beatrix Potter fabric

Meet Bobbie McClure Long

Although Bobbie was born in the northern panhandle of West Virginia and graduated from high school in southeastern Ohio, she has lived most of her life in Pennsylvania. She comes from a long line of quilters and/or seamstresses and owns several family-made antique quilts. Her grandmothers, mom, and aunt were all talented in many different forms of needlework. They would be very pleased she has continued on a road they have traveled.

Making things has always been a part of her life. Beautiful clothes made for her by her mother and aunt were the norm, and quilts were on the beds of her home as she was growing up. Bobbie continued that tradition by making clothes for her daughters when they were young. As her kids grew up, they were surprised to learn that everyone's mom didn't do that. Even then, Bobbie's best work was in the embellishments and details.

She stopped sewing for many years when her very old, dependable White sewing machine was replaced by a new "modern" sewing machine that never worked right and drove her crazy! In 2005 her husband, Tom, said, "I'm sure there have been a lot of improvements in sewing machines. Why don't we just look?" Three sewing machines later, upgrading one machine at a time, she was hooked on quilting and her yo-yo dolls were born.

She has gone from asking if it was OK to have her quilt square look more like a rectangle than a square, to having quilts win multiple ribbons at regional quilt shows and travel with national exhibits. In addition, she enjoys photography, computer graphic arts, and painting, all of which she sometimes includes in her quilts.

I wanted to make a doll that looked like me. I knew I had succeeded when my four-year-old twin granddaughters exclaimed together, "It's you, Grandma!"

She is happily married to her best friend, Tom. They live in the Pocono Mountains of northeastern Pennsylvania with their grand-dog, Juno. Bobbie has four adult daughters; three sons-in-law; four adult stepsons; four stepdaughters-in-law; and between Bobbie and Tom they have twelve grandchildren.

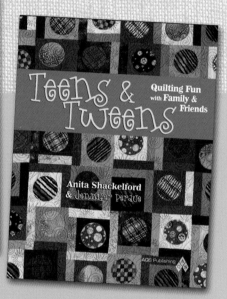